Head in the Clouds
Recollections of an Airline Brat

Rebecca Newlin

Head in the clouds: Recollections of an airline brat
BY REBECCA NEWLIN

Print ISBN: 978-1-54394-962-9
eBook ISBN: 978-1-54394-963-6

Copyright 2018

First Printing September 2018

Published by BookBaby

7905 North Crescent Blvd.
Pennsauken, NJ 08021

www.BookBaby.com

PRINTED IN THE UNITED STATES OF AMERICA

THIS BOOK IS DEDICATED TO MY WONDERFUL
HUSBAND, BILL NEWLIN, WHO SHARED SO
MANY OF THESE ADVENTURES WITH ME AND
CONTINUES TO DO SO TODAY. HE IS MY WORLD!

———————

TO CAROL SVEILICH, ROBERT GOODMAN, AND
JENNIFER BRADLEY FOR THEIR HELP WITH ENDLESS
QUESTIONS, BOOK COVER DESIGN, AND EDITING.

———————

TO TOM BORBA, A FRIEND AND CLASSMATE, WHO,
WHEN I WROTE SOMETHING ON FACEBOOK ABOUT
AN ANECDOTE THAT HAPPENED ON AN AIRPLANE, HE
POSTED, "YOU OUGHT TO WRITE A BOOK." SO I DID.

———————

AND TO FLIGHT ATTENDANT, ALFRED G. MARCHAND,
WHO PERISHED IN THE 9/11 ATTACK. HE WAS A
KIND MAN WHO I DIDN'T KNOW THAT WELL, BUT HE
TOUCHED MY HEART WHEN I HEARD HE WAS ON THAT
ILL-FATED FLIGHT. HE WOULD OFTEN STOP BY MY
CUBICLE AND SAY HELLO. RIP.
THIS STILL HAUNTS ME TO THIS DAY.

1

HOW IT ALL STARTED

It was a typical brisk, sunny, cornflower-blue-sky day on January 31, 1969. It was also the last day of the semester at the College of San Mateo in San Mateo, California.

I had started junior college at age seventeen due to my late-in-the-year birthday. I was now nineteen years old. Little did I know that I would soon make a decision that would shape my entire life in such a very good way.

I had just completed my second year of junior college majoring in Medical Office Business/Secretarial. My immediate goal was to work in a one- or two-person medical office as a receptionist or assistant. I liked the idea of taking care of people and with a small office, I could take my time with each and every patient who came through the door to see their own doctor. And I had always wanted to wear scrubs. They look so comfortable, don't they? Although in those days, I'm not so sure assistants actually wore scrubs. Their uniforms were along the lines of white nurse uniforms and cute hats. Anyway, I had mentioned to my teacher that I needed to take a break from school and find some work. My plan was to go back to school, maybe at night, to finish my undergraduate degree. I hadn't taken a break from school in years. In elementary school, we always went to summer school (my folks both worked full-time and they wanted us kids to be in school so we wouldn't get into trouble with idle minds and hands). I continued that throughout high school. So taking a break was my plan at the time. I was anxious to make a little money. I had already met the love of my life and was thinking ahead to the day we would be married.

The teacher handed me two pieces of paper. She said, "I have two job leads that might work for you." She warmly put them in my outstretched hand, wished me plenty of luck, and I walked out of the College of San Mateo right into bright sunlight. I was filled with excitement. I looked at both pieces of paper -- one was for a job as a medical secretary in a doctor's office (exactly what I was looking for, right?) -- and the other was for a secretarial job with a major airline at San Francisco International Airport.

Without thinking twice, I balled up the medical secretary paper and tossed it into a receptacle without really knowing why.

The word "airline" just got my full attention. It just sounded so appealing. I was still young and usually not that bold. I kind of surprised myself. This was a rare opportunity. Up to that moment I had never given a thought to working for a major airline. It wasn't even on my radar.

It was a Friday. The job post said, "Call for an appointment." I called immediately and the Employment Department asked me to come in right away. I dressed up a little -- no, I dressed up a lot -- and got myself over to the office in an hour or less. When I was interviewed, they asked me, "We're just curious as to why you aren't applying for a stewardess job." (That's what they called flight attendants in 1969). I told them honestly that I hadn't really thought of it but was very open and willing to try any job that was available. I stood up and they took one look at me, and said, "Whoa, you are pretty tall." What? I was 5' 9-1/2" at the time (a little shy of the 5' 10-½" I was going to be). I was nineteen years old and still growing. The airline had smaller aircraft at the time, and I exceeded the height maximum of 5'9". That would later change as the airline ordered wider-bodied aircraft and taller narrow-bodied aircraft, and then the height maximum became 6'1". Of course, timing is everything and I don't regret one moment of working in the maintenance end of the airline business. I learned so much and met so many interesting people along the way.

I interviewed for a secretarial position at the airline's Maintenance Operations Center (MOC). They ushered me over to the medical office for an immediate physical. I got the job right on the spot, because I cleared the physical. Talk about one-stop shopping. I was to report on the following Monday, February 3, 1969. I went home exhilarated. I was going to work for an airline! Little did I know then that I would work there until I retired thirty-five years later at age fifty-five, with two pensions. Along the way, I somehow checked a box on an insurance policy that said "annuity". So in addition to my pension check from the airline, I also get a small, but very welcome, annuity from an insurance company. Also, little did I know how much fun it would be, how hard I would work, and how many amusing, interesting and different jobs I would have over the years. And the travel! Oh my. I hadn't even thought about that aspect yet. At that point, I hadn't ever been on an airplane. My family always traveled by car when my sister and I were growing up. But I could tell it was going to be fun. For the first time, I had my head in the clouds. Up, up and away. I was dizzy with anticipation.

I was so excited. On Sunday night I was with my folks at the dinner table (I was still single and living at home) when I got a call from my new office-to-be. A voice said, "We know you start work officially tomorrow morning, but could you come in tonight and work some overtime? We have a big typing project that needs to be done by Monday morning and the regular secretary is on vacation. If you could work Sunday night, it would really help us out." Well, I'm certainly not going to decline, right? And who ever heard of working overtime before you even started a job? But I did it, and they were so appreciative.

Sunday evening I went into a nearly empty office and one person handed me a large handwritten package that needed to be typed and gave me special instructions. She left me her telephone number in case I had questions, but otherwise left me alone to do the typing project. In fact, I think she left for the evening. I've always been a good typist, so it wasn't daunting. I worked on it for several hours and when I was done with the project, the guard downstairs let me out of the building. I always felt safe there. There was always a guard on duty checking people in and out and I knew it was a safe place to work. The next morning I started my first full day on the job and I wasn't nearly as nervous as I would have been, had I not worked the night before. At least I knew my way around a little.

*   *   *   *   *

My monthly paycheck in 1969 was maybe $300 per month. I cashed my very first paycheck. I had big bills and little bills. I spent it here and there until eventually I was down to fifty-one dollars. So one Sunday, I went to church in the back of the valley and thought I put a dollar in the collection basket. I then went to gas up my car, which cost a whopping $.25 per gallon at the time. I recognized a guy from high school who was pumping gas. Wanting to impress him, I whipped out what I thought was a $50 bill to pay for my meager gas bill. I only had $1. What? So I must have put $50 in the collection basket. Oh my. This meant I was covered at church for a long while. But with egg on my face, I had to go back to the gas station with more money to finish paying for my gasoline.

After that, because I was living at home with my parents and didn't need much money, I would get my paychecks and put them in a drawer. Finally, one day our Chicago office telephoned me at work and asked me to cash some of my paychecks so they could adjust their billing. I was screwing up the payroll system by not cashing my checks.

*   *   *   *   *

I wasn't married at the time, but since my future husband Bill was such a big part of my airline life, here's how we met. As juniors in high school, we were off for the summer, and we would be starting our senior year in September at different high schools. It was June of 1966 and my girlfriend and I decided to go to a dance at the College of San Mateo. This was pretty exciting for a high schooler. A college dance! Some group named The Byrds was playing there that evening. Yes, *those* Byrds, who went on to fame and fortune. My friend danced with a nice guy who had a friend with him. That friend was Bill. I was dancing with another young man named John. John and I ended up dancing all evening and then going out now and then for a couple of months. But he was in college and was gone a lot of the time.

In the meantime, our school's homecoming dance was coming up. I was the senior high school class president, but I didn't have a date. In those days a bunch of girls or guys didn't attend the parties or dances as a group like they do nowadays: everyone had to be asked out on a date. So I asked my girlfriend to ask her boyfriend to ask his friend (Bill), who had attended the dance that night in June, to call and ask me out. I didn't recall much about him except that he was tall. This young man, Bill, called me up and asked to take me to my own homecoming dance. I said yes, of course. This nice young man arrived one evening (November 18, 1966) in a sports coat and slacks and a tie to meet me and my parents. At this same time, my sister and her then-fiance had asked a pot-and-pan sales-man from "Wear Ever" to come to their home to show the latest in pots and pans. He brought two trainees along with him. In our living room that evening sat four young men dressed in sports coats, slacks and ties. I'm sure Bill at first wondered, "What's going on in this house? Is this an Escort Service?" I came out and looked around at all four of these young men and without knowing which guy was my blind date, I said, "Mom, I'd like you to meet Bill Newland" (our last name is actually Newlin, but what did I know - I hadn't met him yet.) I waited for someone, anyone, to stand up so I would know which one was my date. There was a long, awkward pause, or so it seemed. Then Bill stood up and I finally knew who I was dating that evening. He would later joke that if he had never stood up, he might have had a wonderful career as a pot-and-pan salesman!

We had a lovely evening and I thought he was a kind gentleman and very likable. I had hoped to see him again. The first thing I noticed about him was his gorgeous hazel eyes and his forearms. He was seventeen, but he had "man" forearms. I later found out he was an avid surfer, and he still is to this day. He paddled out to go surfing almost daily, so that's probably why his forearms were so muscular. So grown up, I thought. We fell in love soon after that. We got engaged three years later, then married in 1970. We will celebrate our forty-eighth wedding anniversary this August. I've now known this wonderful guy for fifty-two years. And the best friend who was with him at the college dance became the Best Man in our wedding. To this day, I have a little regret that my girlfriend (who I was with that night of the college dance) was not in my wedding. She attended the wedding as a guest, but she was such a big part of our getting together, that I now wish she had been "in" the wedding. She once told me that introducing me to Bill, "was one of the best things I've ever done". I think so too.

* * * * *

My FIRST FREE STANDBY TRAVEL TRIP AS AN AIRLINE EMPLOYEE WAS WITH MY DEAR PARENTS TO WASHINGTON, D. C. I knew it might be the last trip I would take with them as an unmarried daughter. My parents also got travel privileges because I was under twenty-one and because I was living at home with them. So we flew on a pass and my mom was so proud of me working for the airline. Now technically my position was a "Job Group 2" and I was a roving stenographer/file clerk/secretary. There was no such thing as a "Job Group 1" for some strange reason. Maybe it was so employees didn't feel like they were hired at rock bottom.

Eventually my mom and dad are with me at the podium checking in for a flight. The gate agent asked us which one was the employee? My mom puffed up and said, "That's my daughter, she is an executive with the airline". My mom always, and I mean always, made me feel bigger and better than I really was. Her belief in me really shaped how I turned out as an adult. So off we went to Washington, D. C. and what a good trip it was. We visited all of the historic sites that we could see, and I even walked up the entire stairs to the top of the Washington Monument. Can you even imagine doing that at age 68? Yeah, I'll bet I could still do it -- as long as I don't have to prove it! And as for the flight itself, all three of us got into the first-class cabin. My mom and dad were seated to my right and I was sitting on the left-hand side of the plane. I looked over at my parents enjoying the lovely service and food and champagne and it bought tears to my eyes. I was so glad to be doing something for them. They continued to travel in the United States and Europe until about ten years before they passed away. I sure do miss them.

*　*　*　*　*

WITHIN SIX MONTHS OF WORKING AT THE AIRLINES, MY NOW HUSBAND AND I GOT ENGAGED, AND ONE AND A HALF YEARS LATER, WE GOT MARRIED. Yes, we were young, but he was in the military and I had a full-time job. Around that time, some of my single friends were buying the latest fun tee shirts that said "Marry me, fly free." Someone thought that was a clever tee shirt to have single airline employees wear. I didn't have to get one, thankfully. Free travel was a perk that employees and their eligibles had the privilege of getting. And that shirt is probably a great conversation starter at a party or at the bar (not that I would know firsthand).

Now, as employees, and employee eligibles, we almost always rode on a pass. We are called "SA's" (space available), "non-rev's" (non-revenue), pass riders, standby's, or airline employees. That's where you stand by, and wait until all customers are on board. If there is a seat or two available, and you are the most senior, you may be offered boarding at no cost to you. We always considered this to be an adventure and a privilege. Yes, there were times when we saw several flights come and go, while we continued to stay put in the boarding area. Some times we just had to go home for the day as we couldn't get on any flights to anywhere. While in the boarding area, my husband and I would play our own original game called "looks like." Our made-up rules were to watch the gates, where someone gets off of a flight and we say to one another, "looks like....Robin Williams" (as an example). We would either say, "oh wow, no kidding," or "no way." It was a fun way to pass the time. Sometimes it was the actual celebrity. "Looks like Danny Glover" Wait, it IS Danny Glover! We saw celebrities galore, including Robin Williams, Danny Glover, David Ogden Stiers, B. B. King, Patti

LaBelle, Kanye West, Loni Anderson, Ethel Kennedy, Susan Saint James, and many others, including many members of the Lawrence Welk show. They were in the boarding area all together, going to, I'm guessing, Las Vegas. They all looked so squeaky clean and well groomed. That is what first made me look their way. Then I recognized them from the television show.

*　*　*　*　*

FAST FORWARD TO A FEW YEARS LATER, I WAS WORKING MY DAY JOB AS A SECRETARY WHEN MY BIG BOSS ASKED ME TO GO DOWN-STAIRS AND ESCORT THE NEW ENGINEER UP TO HIS NEW OFFICE. So I walked downstairs and who did I see but John, the young man I had dated at the College of San Mateo dance and for a short while after. We laughed when we saw one another. We were now both married and I was going to be his secretary. We often talked about double dating with our respective spouses but we never got around to actually doing it. Then he left our company to go to another aviation company, getting a nice promotion.

I ended up working at the Maintenance Operations Center for 21 years – as a secretary, roving stenographer, personnel representative, employment representative, human relations representative, and some various temporary assignments. A roving stenographer was someone who would fill in when other secretaries were on vacation or were otherwise not at work. It was also that "Job Group 2" that I had previously mentioned. Okay, I was hired at the lowest job grade the company had, but that was fine with me. I was nineteen. You had to start somewhere. I "roved" to engineers' offices, took shorthand from an engineer or two and transcribed my notes and typed them up for the engineers in the vast office. There were rows and rows of engineers and engineering technicians. A lot of the text was airline jargon that I did, in time, become very familiar with. I remember the first time I typed the name of a big airplane manufacturer that first overtime evening. I typed MacDonald Douglas instead of McDonnell Douglas. Luckily, before the end of that first evening, I saw it typed out correctly somewhere else and made the changes before turning in my typewritten report. Otherwise, my employment might not have lasted thirty-five years.

Another time, an engineer had written out the statement, "yaw damper inoperative" (a term having something to do with flight controls). I could hardly read his writing, and I typed "your damper's inoperative." Seriously? Luckily, I did not do that often, and finally got used to the airline jargon. But the engineers sure got a kick out of that. I would also read their handwriting (some of it was very bad. What were they, doctors?) I would circle in red the words I couldn't make out. Then I would give it back to them and they could correct or interpret it for me before I typed it up. For every letter written, there had to be a correspondence file copy made. It was usually listed like this: C-00-11-22, as an example. So after circling the unclear words in red and not seeing a correspondence file number, I wrote "C- " on the top of the page so they could insert the correct file number. One young engineer came up to me with his marked-up copy and said, "Teacher, I only got a C- on my paper? I thought it was better than that."

While working in Engineering Files, we filed some of those correspondence files I just mentioned. We also filed engineer's drawings (vellums) of various aircraft parts and assemblies on various aircraft. I recall filing vellum drawings of Caravelle aircraft parts. I had never even heard of a Caravelle aircraft as it had already been taken out of service by the time I started working there in 1969. Clearly there was a backlog of filing to be done. I can only imagine an office where a stash of filing was stuffed somewhere by someone "to do later" and then forgotten. I didn't mind filing as others did. The file cabinets were tall and I could stand up and do the filing, instead of sitting in a chair all day.

There were six of us worker bees in that office and surprisingly, we all got along famously and we worked for a very nice boss. It was there that I met, and worked alongside, the youngest grandmother I had ever known. She had become pregnant at thirteen and had a daughter. Her daughter grew up and had become pregnant when she was also thirteen. So this co-worker, a very dear person really, was a twenty-six year old grandmother. I couldn't even imagine such a thing, but I knew it was entirely possible.

She and I were often pulling pranks. Like the one time we traded badges and walked into the security office and had to show the guards our badges. She was an African-American lady with a huge afro. I had long straight brunette hair at the time. So we walked into the office and I flashed her badge and she flashed mine. The Guard just laughed, and said "Oh, you two."

One Monday morning, a very important meeting was called. We six co-workers gathered around our boss and she seriously announced that her dog had puppies over the weekend -- six to be exact -- and then she laughed and said we were all getting one! What could I do? Everyone else was going to take one. Six weeks later, I got this teeny tiny little German Shepherd/Scottish Deerhound to bring home to my mom and dad's house. Did I mention that the tiny puppy grew to be a giant dog who weighed 125 pounds? The puppy, Zachary, was so lonely at home all day all by himself. And we certainly did not want to get him a companion dog. We could barely manage one. It was all I could do to feed him and exercise him. Bill would sometimes drive down Linda Mar Boulevard in Pacifica in his Volkswagen bug with Zachary running after him on the sidewalk, two miles down to the beach – and two miles back. Zachary would barely break a sweat. I think that there are leash laws nowadays that say you cannot have a dog running down the sidewalk like that but what did we know back then? At the time, you could just let dogs out at the beach and let them run all over the beach and trample people, terrorizing them.

Zachary was the last dog I ever had. It wasn't his fault. He was unruly and untrained because we had precious little time to train him properly. One time we came home from work and he had run down the middle of the boulevard with his long leash flying. He had a section of pipe attached to it. He had pulled out the long leash from the outside faucet. He also took some sections of water pipe with him. He had just taken off for some freedom. His long deerhound ears flapped in the breeze. When we gathered him, the pipe and the leash, we came home to find water spewing out the side of the house. Zachary had ripped the faucet right out of the wall.

Then he got hungry one day and went to our next-door neighbors' home, busted through the open kitchen door and grabbed a steak that they had just barbequed, right off a plate. When it came crashing to the floor, Zachary had also broken the plate. And it was an heirloom plate. Of course! I ran to the supermarket to get our neighbors a new steak but the damage had been done. I couldn't replace their heirloom plate. They did like Zachary, however, so it ended as well as could be expected. That neighbor worked at the cafeteria at our high school, and she always had a wonderful cooking aroma around her. One day we found Zachary right by her side at the high school waiting to get a treat. We had no idea how he busted out of the fence surrounding our house. He was so tall he probably just stepped over it.

A short while later, thankfully, a friend in Bodega Bay told us he needed to find a deerhound to help out on his farm, rounding up deer, I suppose. We brought Zachary up to the ranch and he literally jumped out of the car and took off running the full length of the ranch, again with those same floppy ears flapping in the breeze. Imagine a police dog with floppy ears. We never saw him again but he was where he was destined to be, in the fresh air and ample fields to run in. And he finally had someone who had time to care for him. I don't think I ever mentioned to my boss that we no longer had the "Big Z". There was no need to. As I mentioned, we never got another dog. While we missed Zachary, it was for the best.

* * * * *

AROUND EASTER ONE YEAR WHILE WORKING AT THE MAINTE-NANCE OPERATIONS CENTER, A KIND AND THOUGHTFUL ENGINEER GAVE ME A FIVE POUND SEE'S CANDY EASTER EGG (CHOCOLATE COVERED WITH FIVE POUNDS OF MY FAVORITE NOUGAT INSIDE). It was decorated beautifully and covered with a saran type wrapping. It was so pretty to look at. Now I have very little self-control with See's candies, but I placed that stunning five-pounder on my small kitchen table at home as a centerpiece. Day after day went by and the entire time, that huge Easter egg sat on my table. On Easter Sunday, my husband mentioned that he was very impressed with my self-control -- the Easter egg was still intact. I sheepishly said, "Well, yeah…." And then he picked it up! It was a five ounce shell by now! I had been hollowing out the nougat from underneath and placing the saran wrap neatly back on the egg, preserving the thin candy shell. Busted! But those daily tablespoons of creamy nougat were awesome. We had a good laugh about that, but Bill was right. I really did have little self-control when it came to See's candies.

Speaking of See's candies, our offices were located in South San Francisco very nearby to a See's candy store/warehouse. Apparently some candies, when made, come out looking less than perfect and sometimes two candies stuck together. Those were called "seconds" and not suitable for those lovely layers of candies that you see in the pretty boxes in a See's candy store. The "seconds" were bagged in plain brown lunch bags, stapled shut, and sold by the hundreds to eager airline employees and other companies nearby. Someone would give the call, "The See's Seconds are here!" We ran to the lobby nearly trampling one another, and we bought several bags for our office mates and ourselves. They tasted just as good as the pretty ones and we got a great deal. The bags were about $1 a bag and that wasn't even a lot of money back then.

*   *   *   *   *

From day one in the engineering department, I was known as becky. Then when I was in my thirties, I discovered that our company had started covering orthodontics on our dental plan. I had a big space between my teeth and thought I always needed braces. So I decided to get them, which I wore confidently for a year and a half. There is something about being self-conscious while wearing braces when you are eleven or twelve, but when you are in your thirties, you are doing it for yourself and not for your parents. I had corrected my teeth on my own dime, and with that came confidence. That is, except when someone watched you eat an Oreo cookie while wearing braces and then made you laugh. There was no hiding that chocolate cookie smeared all over your braces. Or having your braces go "sproing" and having them come off after having a martini. The alcohol dissolved the glue. (I had to go back to the Orthodontist). Also at that same time, I had taken classical piano at a local college in the evenings. Shortly after, I was transferred to the Turbine Shop, a couple of buildings away. My boss went over there to be the new department director and I wanted to go with him. He was a great boss. Just for fun, on a whim, I decided I would introduce myself as Rebecca since I was now feeling like a grown-up. My braces were finally taken off, and I was now a piano player. It sounded foreign coming out of my mouth when I first introduced myself, but the name stuck. "Rebecca" was what I was known as from then on. The name change helped me remember who I knew when. If someone called me Becky at work, I knew it was someone from my previous jobs in the other building. I remain Rebecca to this day but I answer to Becky or Becca. Oh, and my teeth are still straight but I stopped taking piano lessons and cannot play piano today to save myself. Where, again, is middle C?

* * * * *

CARPOOLING WAS BIG EVEN IN THE 70S. A friend of ours who was an engineering technician at the Maintenance Operations Center, had a large van with roof racks that looked like Bullwinkle's horns, you know, the cartoon character. So we fondly called the van Bullwinkle. He would drive and round up a motley crew of co-workers. We would ride from Redwood City and Belmont to the San Francisco airport and back again. We would laugh and tell stories some days and other days we'd just nap or read and not talk much at all. Usually the rides home on Friday afternoons were the most spirited. Here comes the weekend!

Now, I am a stickler for being on time. I always have been on time and hopefully always will be. I believe in the saying – "If you are on-time, you are late." If you are fifteen minutes early, you are on time. That said, one morning I heard the van horn. I was still asleep in bed! Oh noooo. I went to the door of our apartment in my robe, sans eye makeup and with major bed head. I waved them on and told them I was sorry that I had overslept. That only happened once but I was mortified. I still managed to get up, shower, and drive myself to work that day. I wasn't even a minute late.

Friends know about my promptness. We have been known to drive around the block a couple of times in their neighborhood waiting for the clock to strike 5:00 p.m. or whatever time the invitation said to arrive. And when it strikes 5:00 p.m., there we are knocking on their door. I overheard one friend say through the front door, "It's exactly 5:00 p.m., it must be the Newlin's." When I have my own dinner party, I expect someone to knock on my door promptly at least by 5:00 p.m., give or take a minute. That's just me. My hubby asked me why we always had to be the first to arrive and the last to leave? I answer, "Because it's a party, that's why."

Yes, carpooling was a big thing. With so many people working at the airport, there was an abundance of parking spaces. These spaces were really far away so carpooling made sense. I started carpooling with another gal who lived nearby in El Granada, California. We chatted about a lot of things driving to and from work. One thing that really intrigued me was that her husband was a P-51 Mustang pilot. He had his own airplane in the hangar at the Half Moon Bay Airport. I thought that the P-51 Mustang was a pretty cool rocket ship of an airplane. I also thought it would be fun to fly in one. I mentioned it to her and she mentioned it to her hubby. So one morning on my day off during the week, I was in bed and I heard someone knocking on the door. Well I couldn't answer the door as I wasn't dressed or presentable. Boy, did I blow that opportunity! It was her husband knocking on the door. He was on his way to his hangar to take the P-51 Mustang out for a spin and he was going to take me along. I learned about it a few days later when Polly and I carpooled together. Right place, wrong time.

WHEN WE LIVED IN MONTARA, CALIFORNIA (OUR FIRST HOME), I WAS STILL WORKING IN THE MAINTENANCE OPERATIONS CENTER. Several of the engineers had airline-related hobbies like flying private airplanes, hang gliding, or remote control airplane flying. One engineer had a plane he rented often from the San Carlos Airport, inexpensively, since he was a member of The Flying Club. It was a Cessna 172. He had taken us out in the plane before and we would fly either from San Carlos Airport or Half Moon Bay Airport and go somewhere for lunch – and back. What an enjoyable way to spend a sunny day. He was in the process of getting "rated" where you have to land without looking, using instruments only. Oh my goodness, he is preparing to land the plane, Bill and I are in the plane with him, and he dons a hood so he can only see the instruments as he is landing! I was more than a little worried but we made it just fine. He even let me take the controls once for just a short while. I was amazed how quickly the airplane responded to the slightest movement of my hands on the controls. After that experience, I thought briefly about taking flying lessons, but it was as costly as racing cars, maybe more so. I never pursued it.

Another day, a friend and Bill and I, were at our house painting our bathroom. In the 70s, stripes and shapes and curved lines were a trend. It was around the same time that the wonderful artist, Peter Max, was all the rage. Many of us amateurs were painting and taping boldly to come up with something wild and colorful like his artwork. We masked and taped off shapes and sizes and got different colors of paints stirred and ready to paint (What where we thinking?) Our pilot friend called us on the telephone and said "Drop everything. I'm in Half Moon Bay, want to go for an airplane ride?" So we dropped everything and went for a ride. There were four of us in the plane and we had a great time, until we flew over Stanford University. Our friend asked our pilot "What is that below us?" "Stanford," the pilot said. "Want to see it better?" With that, he dipped a wing and lowered his elevation. It seemed like we had plummeted and then wildly pulled back up. We got a better look at it, all right. I looked over at our painter friend, and he was green. "Uh oh, I think we need to turn back." We got home just in time. He was still green. He didn't want to paint anymore.

* * * * *

ONE OF THE FIRST THINGS WE DID WHEN WE WERE NEWLY MARRIED WAS TO BUY A WORLD GLOBE. It sounded like a good thing to do since I worked at an airline. I really needed to be more aware of where cities and countries were. I enjoyed geography but I didn't know all of the areas in the world. When you are young and don't have a ton of money, but you get free tickets to almost anywhere, there is such a joy about the task of picking out places to travel. When we were ready to go on a vacation, we spun the globe and put one finger down as it was slowing down. Where the finger landed was where we were going to travel on that particular vacation. One time it landed on Geneva, Switzerland. Another time my finger landed on Saginaw, Michigan. Bill said something like "let's try for two out of three." Yes, it shaped where we traveled for many years. And it was such a blast. We are such airline brats.

* * * * *

AT SOME POINT, I BECAME THE SECRETARY TO THE DIRECTOR OF ENGINEERING. He was a wonderful boss and I so enjoyed working with him. In those days, we went out to lunch with a few people in the office occasionally. That was in the days of one-to-two martini lunches. However, I was still only twenty years old. He would always ask me if I had turned twenty-one yet. I would say no, and order myself a diet soda. One day at lunch, I announced that I was now twenty-one years old. "Let me order you a drink," he says. Okay. He ordered me a Tanqueray gin martini with a twist, straight up. It was very good. And I only had one so that I could still type when I got back to the office, not having had much experience with adult beverages. And in true engineering form, he said, "Never get an olive, it displaces too much liquid and you get less of the beverage. The twist of lemon is placed on the rim of the glass so that no liquid is displaced." Definitely an engineer. Well, I never knew that. But I do love olives! I still order that special drink occasionally when we dine out, just to remember him and make a toast to him.

*   *   *   *   *

At the airlines, we got our usual holidays off. In addition, you got to take your birthday off. Who wouldn't want to have an extra special day off? It was a genuine holiday and you could take it either on your birthday or on another day. So I told my boss one afternoon that I was going out with a couple of co-workers for Mexican food for lunch. "Have a good time," he said. I just wanted him to know that I would be gone a little longer than the usual half hour we would normally get. After a pitcher of margaritas shared with a couple of people, and a very full belly of Mexican food, I just couldn't go back to the office. I just wanted to go home and take a nap. I called my boss and asked if I could take the rest of the day off for my birthday holiday. He said, "....but you've already worked half of the day, so you are only getting a half day off". I told him that was okay with me. I went home and took a nap. He was a very good boss indeed. And I always got my work done on time.

My boss reported to the big vice president, whose offices were known as the "Taj Mahal" to many of us. The office row was so elegant. It was enclosed in glass and just had a different vibe when you walked in there. It was sort of like walking into a church and starting to whisper out of reverence. One day I was asked to sit in for the secretary of the vice president, as the regular secretary was out sick. There was a big meeting going on in the vice president's office. Now I thought I always dressed fairly well for work, but this particular day I was dressed down – a denim blue jean dress and I had blue fingernail polish on to match it. Not exactly what the vice president's secretary in the Taj Mahal would wear, but it was the way it was. And I wasn't given much notice that I had to fill in for her. So all the bigwigs in the Maintenance Operations Center gathered for the meeting in the vice president's office. Halfway through the meeting, my regular boss comes out and asks me if I could get coffee for everyone. Yikes, how do I do that? Who wants sugar or cream, or just black coffee? I had never been asked to do this before. But I did find a trolley and a pot of coffee and I set it up nicely with sugars, cream, stir sticks, and cups. Then I headed for the vice president's office. I was nervous, but I had to go in. I knocked on the door, opened it, and proceeded to roll the trolley over a threshold. I bumped it and everything got knocked on the floor. There I was in my denim dress and blue fingernails, on my hands and knees in this luxurious office, picking up everything I could. I sheepishly rolled the cart back out to try it again. There was a little nervous chuckling, and as I backed out of the office, I heard my own boss say, "Who was that person?" Well at least it broke the ice and I wasn't nervous the second time I went in. I held my head high, and walked in with the coffee trolley. And I did it successfully I might add.

* * * * *

THE MAINTENANCE OPERATIONS CENTER WAS LIKE ITS OWN CITY. We had restaurants (well, cafeterias really), a store where you could buy coffee mugs, airplane models, airline related gifts, among many other things. We had the business offices, the mechanics area, storekeeper area (where they kept track of airplane parts), hangars where the airplanes were parked, credit unions, and travel desks. You could do what you needed to do in a given day or on your lunch half hour or breaks, without ever leaving the base. I frequented the credit union and the travel desk quite often. They were so knowledgeable and could answer most of your questions on money and travel. Our credit union manager was like my second mom. I would go in to consolidate the several credits cards that I had going all at once and she would admonish me for racking up so much debt on so many cards. I would swallow (gulp) and tell her I'd try to do better. Then a year or so later, I would show up again for the same reason, and she would say (kindly, of course) "you racked up more credit card debt? What am I going to do with you?" I guess her money management education finally took hold because now that we are both retired, we have one credit card and we pay it off in full every month. And we own our home outright (no mortgage). She would be proud.

We also had a payroll department upstairs where you could go to if you had a problem with your paycheck. One day, the word got out that one of the payroll clerks was wearing "hot pants" like the stewardesses wore on PSA (Pacific Southwest Airlines). Short shorts! In the business office! We all took turns running upstairs to see for ourselves. It was pretty scandalous in those days.

The hangars themselves were a treat to see and walk around on your lunch half hour. In my 20s, it was not uncommon to hear wolf whistles when you walked by the mechanics. It was actually flattering in those days. It continued on in my 30s. Then one time in my 40s, I walked by some mechanics and I heard a wolf whistle. Before I puffed up like a peacock, I looked behind me. I'm happy that I did. There was someone in their 20s behind me. That's who they were whistling at. Fickle mechanics.

Our airline had contracts with private companies and their airplanes. One time, our airline worked on an airplane that belonged to a royal person from somewhere in the Middle East. I don't remember who he was or which country he was from, but I sure do remember the airplane. The mechanics would let us go onboard if they were working on another part of the airplane and we wouldn't be in their way. I recall a stunning elegant looking interior with gold everywhere – gold faucets in the bathroom, anything normally metal was gold, it seemed. What a treat for the eyes! And then there was the movie "Auntie Mame" starring Lucille Ball. The production company had their own plane! And our mechanics were servicing it. So that was pretty special too. It was very lavish. Boy, that goes way back in time.

In the 1970s there were transsexuals, of course, but you
didn't hear much about them then. I had my first experience with
that at the Maintenance Operations Center. There was a male airframe and
powerplant mechanic working in the hangars. Word was going around that
he was transitioning to a woman. Women mechanics were rare at the time,
as were women engineers. But there were a few. I believe this man was
very brave to do this. So many months later, we now had a new woman
mechanic around the hangar area. I once ran into her in the ladies room
and she was very nice and we talked a little. What I marvel at is that even
way back then, she seemed to be accepted by mostly everyone. And in my
opinion, that is how it should be.

Since we were now hiring more and more female mechanics, I was
working on some issue as a personnel representative. At the time, male
mechanics would often have pictures of topless women in their tool box
lids to look at during the day. If it's all guys working together, perhaps
no one is offended. It might just be what guys do. However, if a female
mechanic is offended by it, it is now a real problem. We had to get the
mechanics to take down the pictures and have training classes on sexual
harassment policies. We were learning so much about what a woman or
man could and could not do to a member of the opposite sex in the workplace. This was in the 70s and 80s.

* * * * *

An engineer had just finished working on his thesis for
graduate school and he asked me to type up his paper. He
said he would pay me for doing so. I thought about it and figured I could
work on my typewriter in the office after hours, so I said yes. He mentioned
something about my needing to get a certain grade and weight of paper to
type it on. He also said that his thesis had to contain a great deal of Greek
symbols. He even provided me with a Selectric ball with Greek symbols.
This was a metal typeface that clicked in and out on the top of the type-

writer. In those days, I was used to working on a Selectric typewriter, but only with one font and just with the English alphabet. But this new fancy schmancy ball had different fonts and different symbols. You typed up a sentence or two and when you got to the Greek symbol, you stopped, took out the "ball" from the typewriter and inserted the Greek one. Then you typed the one symbol, stopped again, and took out the Greek symbol ball. This went on each and EVERY time you switched from the regular type to Greek symbols. And there were tons of Greek symbols. To say that this was labor intensive was an understatement. I almost gave up, but I couldn't do that to the engineer who was relying on me to finish it. And in those days, if you made a mistake (a typo), you had to gently erase the ink off the paper without making a hole in it. It had to look near perfect when it was all done. I bought a ream of typing paper and started on it. Hours and hours, days and days, for a few weeks, and it was finally finished and ready to present to the engineer. In my young mind, it seemed like I typed the entire ream of paper because I had worked so hard and long on it. I presented the thesis to him and he paid me for my hard work. Done! Or so I thought. He came back a few days later and told me that he had turned in his thesis and the professor said, "It's typed on the wrong grade of paper. I cannot accept it." I figured paper was paper. But no, when he had mentioned the grade of paper at the beginning, I didn't think it really mattered all that much. Well, it did. I had to type the entire thesis on the correct grade of paper, all over again. And when I was almost done with the thesis, a wise guy engineer got one of those fake white out bottles with a fake puddle of white out that looked like it had spilled out of the bottle and onto my hard work! Oh no! I thought I had to replace some pages and was ready to cry until he told me about the prank. But still, lesson learned the hard way. Today we just type away like crazy and we have auto-correct. Then we save it to the computer and make changes at will. Much easier than in the old days. Thank goodness!

2

DEGREE RECEIVED. NOW ON TO MANAGEMENT JOBS

OVER THE YEARS, I WENT BACK TO SCHOOL AND FINISHED UP MY UNDERGRADUATE DEGREE AS I HAD PLANNED. It took me eighteen years of on and off night school. In between I took piano classes and concert choir classes, or art or something entertaining. This delayed my degree. It was worth it. I wanted to work in management and that was a requirement of any management job the airline had to offer. I've never regretted that one year in 1984 to 1985, when I worked forty hours a week and did school and homework for another forty hours a week. I would come home from work and just delve into school work until I needed to go to sleep. On weekends, I don't recall ever even getting dressed. I just woke up and worked until night time, Saturday and Sunday. Our across-the-street neighbors once commented on it. "Did you bury your wife out in the backyard? We haven't seen her for months." Not sure how I pulled it off, but I did and finished up my undergraduate degree in 1985. I even bought myself a cute little coffee cup which said Class of '85. Mission accomplished.

As promised, once I had my degree (Bachelor of Science in Human Relations and Organizational Behavior) I got my first management job. From there I worked in Personnel, Employment, Human Relations, and other interesting jobs, including some temporary assignments. I worked with Management alongside some of our Union groups – mechanics and storekeepers, mostly. And of course I later became a supervisor of flight attendants.

* * * * *

W HILE GETTING TO KNOW SOME OF THE AIRPLANE MECHANICS,
AND THERE APPEARED TO BE HUNDREDS AND HUNDREDS, IF NOT
MORE, I HEARD A STORY THAT I HOPED TO BE TRUE. It was the late
60s and early 70s and the song, "Incense and Peppermints" was playing
endlessly on the radio. The band who performed it was called the "Strawberry Alarm Clock." The word out on the street was that they were airline
mechanics by day, and rockers by night. Now I had always thought they
were our San Francisco mechanics, but I understand they were formed
in the Glendale, California area. Well, maybe they were the Los Angeles
based airplane mechanics. It was just fun to know someone who knew
someone who knew the band, Strawberry Alarm Clock. Weren't they a
one-hit wonder?

* * * * *

T HERE WAS THIS ONE JOB WHERE I WAS AN EMPLOYMENT REPRE-
SENTATIVE. This was a fun assignment. I would go with a technical
representative to a technical aviation school, recruiting young people for
airframe and powerplant mechanics for the airline. The technical representative was assessing their mechanical knowledge and I would be assessing
their employability. I went to Waco, Texas to recruit some good ol' boys
(and the very occasional girl). Waco was very different from California for
sure. Lots of trucks, lots of rifle racks, and lots of rifles. But we met some
really talented young men and women. The representative that I went with
was a big foodie. So am I! We would have meals together and they were
grand. One restaurant had booths that were really cute little boats standing
up on end with the pointy end (I've never been much of a sailor) on the
top. And we made darn sure we were up early enough to go have a proper
breakfast before recruiting at nearby aviation schools. "The last employment representative that I traveled with didn't like breakfast, and I had to
eat alone. You're a lot more fun," he told me, between bites.

There was another technical representative I traveled with, this time to Boston. He was also a really fun technical representative and very playful. There we were, once we landed, in a field running around with a mason jar in one hand, trying to catch fireflies at nightfall. And I was in a business suit with high heels. He continually smoked a cigar. In those days, you could smoke in public even in indoors. Oh, the smell of that cigar! It was dreadful, but it was his calling card. It was snowing while we were on another trip to Boston, and we checked in and got our rooms next door to one another. The first thing I did was put on my "traveling muumuu" -- a magenta floral, floor length, and very comfy lounger, that I seldom left home without. It was much like the security blankets of our youth. The phone rang; it was Smokey. "Hey, go to your balcony right now, I have something to show you." So I opened my sliding glass door and stepped outside onto the patio, just in time to get a big ol' snowball thrown right in my face. We both laughed and then shut our respective doors for the evening.

*   *   *   *   *

As an employment representative, I was asked to go to Denver for six weeks to help hire pilots. To date, I had not been around pilots much except when on a trip somewhere. I have a lot of respect for these courageous employees who get us from place to place so safely.

Part of my job was to make certain that certain EEOC (The U. S. Equal Employment Opportunity Commission) guidelines were followed to a "T". I was matched up with a very senior, recently-retired airline captain who was doing the recruiting from a technical standpoint. He sure knew what he was doing technically, but he didn't have a flair for the EEOC rules. He was hired in the good ol' days when we didn't give much thought to being politically correct. We were interviewing person after person, when a beautiful young bright woman walks in. Blonde, blue-eyed, petite and quite the commercial pilot, judging from her ample resume. Things were going really well until the retired captain just blurted out, "Honey, I'll bet you can't even reach the pedals." Oh no! I lightly kicked his shin under the table. "What? I can't say that?" Oh my. Afterward we had a good laugh about it, but I politely asked him to be careful with his wording so we don't get sued. "Okay," he assured me.

Then we had an interview with a male pilot. Things were going swimmingly until the interviewee mentioned he was a helicopter pilot. "Helicopters," the retired captain bellowed, "I'll bet you have lace on your shorts!" Crap! I kicked him under the table again, maybe not as lightly as the first time. He said to the nervous interviewee, "She's kicking me under the table, so I must be saying something I shouldn't." But, still, it was a very enjoyable six weeks.

* * * * *

AT THE END OF THE WORKDAY ON BUSINESS TRIPS, THERE WASN'T MUCH TO DO, SO I HAD MY HAIR AND NAILS DONE. Now I rarely get a manicure – a pedicure, yes. But seldom a manicure. I just like to dig my hands in dirt while gardening and doing chores and don't want to have to worry about my hands. But for some strange reason, I got long fake nails put on, and had them painted bright red. They really looked nice and on a long business trip away from home, I didn't have to do any gardening or making beds or anything that would mess them up. Then, one of the co-workers mentioned that he had seen a volleyball net outside and maybe we could get a volleyball game going. I was up for it, but then thought of my newly polished long nails. Oh well. I liked volleyball more than I liked manicures, so I got in on the game. Within fifteen minutes of serving and tossing the ball over the net back and forth, I noticed I had broken most of my nails. I asked one of the guys playing next to me, if he could please put my broken nails in his pocket, in case I could have them repaired later. What did I know? They looked a mess! But we were having fun playing volleyball. Well, I forgot all about my fake fingernails that I had given to the guy to hold for me. I just got them all taken off and went back to my normal, short, comfortable unpainted hands. A week went by and some of us got to go home for the weekend. The same guy approached me after going home and said, "I really had a hard time trying to explain to my wife why I had someone else's red polished fingernails in my pants pocket." That is the last time I ever fooled around with fake fingernails.

Once I had a rare opportunity to recruit some employment candidates for our Alaska offices. I flew to Alaska by myself and never saw daylight. It was dark when I arrived and got settled in my hotel room. On the way up in the elevator I shared the ride with a native Intuit (an eskimo), complete with the fur-lined hooded parka. He was so interesting as I had only seen an authentic native in the movies. And here I was getting to share an elevator with him. In the morning I interviewed people all day in a nice office nearby the airport where, when I looked out of the windows, it was still dark. I enjoyed this business trip and the dark taxi ride back to the airport. I was in awe seeing so much open space and snow. And I even bought a hot dog at the airport before I left. For five dollars! A skinny hot dog on a skinny bun. And this was in the late 80s. It is sure funny the things you remember years later – a lovely native and an expensive hot dog.

*   *   *   *   *

BILL AND I GOT TO BE GOOD FRIENDS WITH A YOUNG MARRIED COUPLE – ONE OF WHOM WAS A STOREKEEPER AT THE MOC. Over the years we traveled together and got into mischief together. Sadly, both of them have since passed away. I decided to have them over for dinner one day. We were all young and not wealthy in those days. I was just going to make spaghetti and serve some inexpensive wine. I was going to make it an airline theme, however. At the time I was working in Aircraft Interiors Engineering, and had access to mock-ups of airplane seats. I inquired about borrowing them, but they could not let me take them home. Shucks! But I did get some things like placemats made out of the carpet that we had on our airplanes. Then I found some hot pads made out of the same material, and some other things that we had out on our airplanes. I had some little menehunes (little Hawaiian guys on a stick) that were used as swizzle sticks in First Class. I took whatever I could legally "borrow." I had it all set up. To make things even more perfect and simple for me, my Swiss-Italian-American dad had recently made up batches of spaghetti sauce and I had several bags of it in our freezer. My Mexican-American mom had also made up batches of chili and I had several bags of chili in our freezer as well. Trouble was I pulled the wrong bag out for the spaghetti. Now, spaghetti sauce is great and chili is great. What is not ideal, however, is when you put chili on spaghetti, thinking it was going to taste like marinara sauce. (Not sure why it didn't work, but it didn't.) We ended up ordering pizza and had a lovely night, and a lot of laughs, as we always did. Well, almost always. Our storekeeper friend was a little moody. If he showed up at our home with a big bright smile, or we showed up at their home, and he answered the door with a wide grin, we knew we were going to have a grand time. If there was no hint of a smile, it was going to be a long, agonizing evening. Luckily, that didn't happen often. We all know people like that, don't we?

Another time with this same couple, they suggested we go to Boston after work on a Friday for dinner! Cool. We got off work, hopped on a plane to Boston and arrived late, but still in time to have a late (really late) dinner. We hailed a cab to a restaurant called "Anthony's Pier Four." We were having fresh fish dinners (crab, lobster, etc.,) around almost midnight, but we were young and carefree and we didn't care. Except for the one gal with us. She ordered fish that came with the head on it and she couldn't eat it because it was looking at her. Again, more laughs. Along the way we telephoned a hotel and got two rooms for the night. We were always traveling "seat of the pants" as we called it, going to an unknown town with no car rental, no hotel, and no dinner reservations. It would make some of our non-airline friends shudder, but it was better than having to cancel and undo everything because you did not get on the airplane as you had hoped and planned for. And it was hard to phone from the airplane, so you would have to wait until you landed to start booking everything once you got there.

After dinner, we settled into our respective rooms in the wee hours and slept in. We got up the next morning, a Saturday, and went to breakfast. Afterwards, we boarded the U.S.S. Constitution for a tour. Later, we took a cab to the airport and flew home late that night. I'm glad we got on that particular return flight. Bill and I were carrying home a live lobster from a fish place (at the airport) that we just had to have. We placed it under our seat and we kept hearing that clickety clack of the live lobster in the carrying case. It kind of made me sad. And when we got home and decided to cook it, I had to leave the room while Bill dropped the lobster into the boiling water. "I heard it scream," Bill said. "Nooooooo, you didn't," I said. I'll never know if he was just kidding me, as I was holding my hands over my ears and had my eyes closed.

* * * * *

BILL WAS (AND STILL IS) A TEASER, FOR SURE. We were getting our blood tests for our marriage license in 1970. We were both getting blood drawn in the same office at the same time. It didn't bother him a bit, but I was just so squeamish about needles in my veins. I was trying desperately not to look. He hollered from the other side of the room, "Look, your blood is green". I fainted.

One weekend, we wanted to take a trip to Los Angeles to visit my in-laws. They lived within walking distance from the Los Angeles airport. Normally we would dress up, take the flight out, and once we were off the airplane, we would run into our respective airport restrooms and change into our Los Angeles garb – flip flops, shorts, and tee shirts. Then we would walk the several blocks to my in-laws' home. We would remain in that style of uniform for the remainder of the trip. That is, until we had to get dressed up for the flight back home. This particular weekend, however, we could not get on a flight all day. We decided to drive from San Francisco to Los Angeles. We packed very little and since we did not have to dress up for a flight, we had only flip flops, tee-shirts, and shorts. Once we arrived at their home, they told us they were taking us out to a very fancy restaurant near Hollywood. This was super cool, but we didn't have clothes packed for a big night out. My in-laws offered to help us out by loaning us some clothes. Now we were in our 20s, but Bill's parents were in their 60s. They had Bill late in life, when they were in their 40s. So I had a house dress from his mom, stockings, and some comfortable and sensible old person's shoes. Bill had a too small sports coat which was way too short in the arm length as well. We looked at one another and chuckled, "We both look like (expletive) clowns." Well, it's only for one night, it would please his folks, and we weren't likely to run into anyone we knew, right? I just wonder what people thought when they saw us. Look at those nice senior citizens with the geeky looking adult kids. Oh, and I just realized that his parents then were probably the age that we are now! What?

* * * * *

Now and then we took weekend trips to Hawaii. We'd leave Friday after work, and we would get there earlier in the day. Hawaii was two or three hours earlier than our time zone. One such time, we were sitting outside around sunset having dinner at a lovely restaurant right on the sand and water in Kona. And just that same day hours earlier, we had been in our respective offices! Then we would leave Sunday night on the "red eye" and fly all night, landing at the San Francisco airport around 6:00 a.m. on Monday morning, with our red eyes! We would head to our apartment in Belmont, shower, and be back to work at 8:00 a.m. Of course, always looking and feeling our very best. Hah! Those trips always left us exhausted on Monday evenings after weekend trips, but we'd go to sleep early. We'd be raring to go by Tuesday. Leaving Hawaii on a Sunday night is pretty daring, so we didn't do that very often. Yes, we had airline privileges, and yes, we were expected to fly on our own time. Oh and yes, we HAD to be at work on time. "I couldn't get on a flight" was not a good enough excuse to come into work late.

Our very first flight to Hawaii was on a 747. Oh, how I loved that giant airplane. We were seated in the Upper Deck Lounge. Just that name alone sounds heavenly and lofty. One other airline had a piano bar up in the Upper Deck Lounge (and just how did they get that piano up there?), but that had to be very luxurious. The flight attendants in those days wore full length Hawaiian muumuu's. They really looked lovely and put you right in the Aloha spirit, even just leaving San Francisco. We had a lovely blonde, petite flight attendant working upstairs on that flight. So there was Bill sitting in his aircraft seat with the cute flight attendant on his lap. I doubt that she was from our San Francisco domicile, because I didn't recognize her, and don't recall seeing her again.

On another trip on a 747, we were seated in the Upper Deck Lounge again. There were four of us employees/eligibles traveling together. We felt so fortunate to all be in the First Class cabin. The call buttons are usually overhead, where you have to consciously reach for the button to summon the flight attendant. This is something that you don't want to do too often. It takes flight attendants away from their time with paying customers. But on this particular configuration, the call button was on the armrest. Oops! The flight attendant came over the first time, and asked us what we needed. "Oh nothing, thanks!" Then it happened again and again. Apparently with every fun story, came a wild arm and hand gesture that rested on the call button with emphasis. After several times that the flight attendant had to come to our seats, I could see her coming our way huffing and puffing with steam coming out her ears. "WHAT NOW?" the flight attendant said. Oops! Sorry, we won't let that happen again. I sincerely hope they changed the location of that call button. Of course, it is a moot point now. Sadly, the Boeing 747 was taken out of service as it was too costly to fly. But it was such a lovely airplane.

Since I was now working in management, Bill and I decided that we would attend a Management Club meeting just to see what they were all about. After working a full day at work, I was reluctant to go home, freshen up, and come back for a couple of hours in the evening to go to a meeting. In fact, we did think about not going. But afterwards, we were glad we went. It was one of those happy hour socials, then a sit down dinner. After dinner, there might have been speeches or maybe a conversation-breaking game of some sort. That evening, we were told that we would participate in a White Elephant gift exchange. You know the one where you are handed a gift and if you don't like it you can trade it once with someone else, if they agree to it. Well, our gift was a yucky looking Gerber's Baby Food jar with strained and mashed spinach or something unknown in it. We tried and tried to give it away to no avail. No one wanted this green sickly looking baby food jar. Certainly not us, as we didn't even have kids to give it to. Maybe even a kid or a baby would turn their nose up at it. I would have if I had a choice. So we thought, oh well, we're pretty stuck with it. We'll just dispose of it after the meeting. After all the exchanges were over with, a management employee walked up to the podium and got on the microphone. He announced the following: "Will the person who has the green Gerber's baby food jar please stand up." I stood up and held it up. He then said, "You have just won two round trip tickets to Ireland on Aer Lingus!" Positive Space! Music to my ears. What an amazing gift. We were elated. Months later we flew on our carrier to New York, then boarded an Aer Lingus jet to Shannon Airport in Ireland. We began our travels to a magical place with some of the nicest people we have ever met. The countryside reminded me of the Land of Oz, it was so green and lush. We stayed in Shannon for a bit, then boarded a train to travel to Dublin. Once in Dublin, we rented a tiny little car, a Toyota Starlit, with right hand drive. Yes, you drove on the opposite side of the road than in the United States. We drove around, stayed at different hotels and visited various museums like the Waterford crystal factory. We had a marvelous time. I found the glass blowing factory especially interesting. When it was my turn to drive this car with a stick shift, every time I had to shift the gears, I would inadvertently roll down the right hand window. And then I would remember to shift the gears with my left hand. It was pretty fun trying to drive around these towns with the little, narrow lanes. On one such street, we were driving down a cobblestone lane and it seemed like the sidewalks were right next to our car door. And the houses were right next to the sidewalks. As we were breezing along, we see a big tour bus coming our way from the opposite direction. Now here we are thinking that there was no way we could both share the road and my eyes grew bigger and bigger as the tour bus approached and the street looked even more narrow. With nowhere else to go, I drove up on as much of the little sidewalk and as far to the left as I could. And we hoped that the tour bus would do the same on the opposite side. Whoosh! They had just breezed by us like the wind. But where was our right side rear view mirror? Laying in the street of course, sheared cleanly off by the big, no make that *huge*, tour bus. We stopped and picked up the remains of the mirror and put them all in the back seat. We then went to the Toyota dealer in town and bought the replacement part and left it next to the broken one in the back seat. When we turned in the car, we explained what had happened and told them we bought the replacement part. No extra charge, they told us. They actually were pleased that we bought the new rear view mirror. It was the least we could do. And I'm guessing that some people would return a wounded rental car without even telling them what had happened.

Later that day, we needed a place to stay for the night and ran across a Tudor style hotel, called the John Barleycorn. That'll do, we thought. Well it was a very nice hotel with a pub, a restaurant, and it boasted that it was a nice setting for a wedding. We knew about the wedding venue because there were a few weddings going on that evening. But wait! It's a Tuesday night. Who gets married on a Tuesday night? We were told it had something to do with a tax break but weren't exactly sure how that worked. There were brides, grooms, and guests galore. Why I remember that the brides had cigarettes dangling from their lipsticked mouths, I have no idea except that mental picture didn't work for me. Not judging, it just didn't look right. Okay, maybe judging a little.

So after settling into our room, we thought we'd go to the pub and have a drink and some pub grub. If you arrived too late to a pub in Ireland and they had stopped making food for the evening, they would say, "Soup's off." I thought at first that they meant it had gotten spoiled sitting out so long. No, they just meant that they had turned off the burner on the stove where the soup was cooking. This pub was a dark, very inviting place to sit and watch television. After being in the pub a half hour, something came on the news about Pacifica, California! That's my hometown. There had been another bad storm. Some houses had started to wash away from a small hillside right on the beach. The houses were just sliding into the ocean. Now at the time, my dear friend was (and is still) living across the street from this disaster. Imagine waking up to find that you now have an unobstructed view of the ocean. It was very sad, but we visited the area as soon as we came home to see the devastation firsthand. There was a lot of caution tape warning people that the hillside was still shaky and not very stable. Over the years, we watched the hillside crumble bit by bit. Many people lost houses and apartments over the years. We often think of our one trip to Ireland with such fondness. We are so grateful for attending that Management Club dinner and winning that trip on that wonderful fateful day.

Oh, we are a diverse group of folks at our airline. We came in all shapes and sizes and colors, I'm happy to say. We all had that common thread – working for an airline and worldwide travelers.

While working in the Turbine shop, some of us had hand held old fashioned pagers attached to the side of our desks. If my boss needed to reach someone "on the floor", I could page that person and he or she would respond with either a phone call or come up in person. "On the floor" was such an interesting way of saying that an employee (usually a mechanic) was working on the first floor of the building, in the turbine shop. "John is on the floor today." Oh, poor thing. I hope he's okay. So any chance we had to page someone on the floor, we would. We would page someone using the sexiest, sultry breathless voices we could muster, and the call would come in almost immediately! We would try out silly voices, baby voices, you name it. Then one day my boss asked me to page a Vietnamese mechanic with a pretty unusual name. So there I was having to say, "Paging Mr. Phuoc Ng". Seriously, I said that on the pager to hundreds of mechanics listening on the floor.

* * * * *

Now, I just happen to be allergic to many things – cats, dogs, dust mites, mold, cigarette smoke, etc. I don't mind it much as long as I don't have to be around it very often or for very long. But I found myself flying to Japan a lot during the time that smoking was still allowed on the airplanes. In Japan, and I know this is a generalization, but it seems that almost everyone smokes. I was on an aircraft with five-across seating in the Economy section. It was the smoking section and I was in the middle. When I couldn't breathe clean air anymore, and was tired of holding a napkin up to my face to block out the smoke, I climbed over a couple of seat mates. I made my way to the back galley to get some fresher air. Wrong! There were many customers lined up back there smoking and socializing. That is something that you cannot get away from, if you are hurtling across the sky on an airplane. Even when you are in the non-smoking section, designated by a placard on the top of the seatback, the row behind you may be the smoking section. What is the point? I spent my entire layover steaming my sinuses in the bathtub with the hottest water I could find. This reminded me of the practice in the 50s of riding around in the family car in the back seat with my sister, my dear asthmatic mother sitting in the passenger seat, and my dad driving, puffing up a storm, with all of the windows rolled up tight. We just didn't know how bad it was for you in those days. I'm beyond thrilled that you can no longer smoke on the airplanes and in the airports. We have come a long way and in a much better direction.

Speaking of smoking, the airport also used to be a smoke-filled airport. People would walk around with their lit cigarettes dangling from their lips. They were in the stores and offices puffing away. When smoking was finally banned in airports, bars, restaurants, and business offices, it wasn't an instant thing. People still lit up out of habit. As we were working the gates, going from flight to flight, we sometimes had to remind people that smoking was no longer allowed indoors. We said this even though we made announcements about it upon landing. I recall being on an airplane where a very nice male flight attendant was making the landing announcement. He started off with the usual announcement as it is shown on our information cards, but he added his own touch to it. He said, "Ladies and gentlemen, please refrain from smoking......for the rest of your lives." I had to smile. If only. Change is hard. But I persisted at asking people to please put out their cigarettes. Yes, I'm a little militant about it. As I mentioned, my dad smoked at home, in the car while driving, with all the windows rolled up and we were trapped inside. And as a result of second hand smoke, I ended up with chronic bronchitis, adult onset allergic asthma, and a smidge of emphysema. So I had no problem asking people to put out their cigarettes. Although I did ask them diplomatically since I was representing the airline. When I mentioned it to Bill, he said that my job description shouldn't be supervisor of onboard services, Job Group 73, but rather smoke detector, Job Group 73! Sometimes upstairs in the office if we worked the swing shift (2:00 p.m. to 11:00 p.m.), a co-worker would say to me, "Hey, I'm going to have a cigarette at my desk, if you don't mind, since it's just you and me working here right now." Nothing doing, I would answer. I stuck to my guns. Buzz kill, I'm sure she thought.

*   *   *   *   *

W<small>E DID HAVE FUN IN THE OFFICE.</small> There were many of us supervisors and thousands of flight attendants. We had operating managers and domicile managers. We worked at least four shifts – approximately 5:00 a.m. to 1:00 p.m., 6:00 a.m. to 2:00 p.m., 8:00 a.m. to 4:00 p.m., 2:00 p.m. to 11:00 p.m. In rare instances, we might work throughout part of the night if a flight was delayed or there was a huge issue going on. There is something so serene about walking through the airport after all of the flights have departed. It's like a ghost town with all of the shops closed down for the evening. There is not a soul in sight, except for the occasional employee or guard. Oh, there might have also been the rare scurry of a little mouse. Eek! It was such a different experience than most of us get, since we usually walk through the airport mid-day. Then there are throngs of people everywhere, running to and from their flights.

One night while leaving work, I saw a flight attendant in uniform sitting alone on a bench in the baggage claim area. She looked like she was in distress. She was newly pregnant and was having a miscarriage right then and there. Our medical offices were already closed for the day, and she had missed her flight home because she couldn't get up and walk to the gate. I'm so glad we found her, as we were able to call the paramedics. They were there immediately to take care of her, poor dear. Imagine having an emergency and not being in your own town, and in an airport that was almost entirely empty.

W<small>E HAD SUPERVISORS WHO WOULD BAKE AND BRING IN GOOD-</small>
<small>IES FOR EVERYONE WHO COULD GET TO IT FIRST (FIRST COME, FIRST</small>
<small>SERVED</small>). We had thousands of employees coming through on a given day. Someone yelled, "I have goodies to share". The employees tumbled out of their tiny cubicles at warp speed to get to the food. When it was someone's birthday, it would be announced at our morning staff meeting. We would trample each other out the door to the break room, after singing Happy Birthday to you, of course. At that time, I had cake batter that I acquired where you had a starter mix, and you just added to the mix almost on a daily basis. So there I was, up early baking what I thought was my only cake, to bring it to the office still warm. Mmmmm, it was good. But I finally had to toss the starter mix because it got to be too much to bake several times a week, week after week, month after month. If we happened to have a meeting with food and had some leftovers, we had a break room where we spread them out. Everyone slipped in and slipped out throughout the day and noshed. Food was such a big part of our office lives.

I and my dear friend and colleague (we started on the same day and went through training together) went downstairs occasionally on our coffee breaks in the morning. We stopped at a restaurant for a cup of coffee and a piece of cornbread. To this day, I think of her whenever I see or smell cornbread.

One day our two operating managers wanted to thank the employees for all of our hard work on some project we were working on. I forget what the project was, but I'll never forget the thank you gift. They donned those paper envelope hats that soda jerks and some restaurant workers wore. They got white lab coats and a rolling cart from one of our airplanes. They filled it with plates, forks, and tons of ice cream. They had a little bell and they walked through the office cubicles, row by row, bell ringing, passing out ice cream to all of us. It was very cute, and very much appreciated. Thank you, Harry and Stephanie.

* * * * *

I HAD TO LAUGH WHEN SOMEONE ASKED ME WHAT AIRLINE I WORKED FOR. When I told them, they'd sometimes ask, "Do you know Suzy Jones? She's a flight attendant out of San Francisco." We have thousands and thousands of flight attendants in that domicile. So, I would usually answer by holding my hand out in front of me, indicating a certain height, and saying "Is she blonde, about this tall, and wears a navy blue uniform?" And nine times out of ten, someone would answer, "Yes, that's her." No, I don't know Suzy Jones. I had between 200 to 700 flight attendants reporting to me. I was hard pressed to know all of them. Why I say that is that some flight attendants came and went on their flights for years without touching base with me or other supervisors. They knew what they needed to do and how to do it. Our main portion of time was spent with the newer hires who had questions about the service flow, or how to do a certain aspect of their job. They needed us more than the senior flight attendants.

When at parties, a good conversation starter is usually something like "Where do you work?" If I said my airline's name, invariably someone would say something nice about a flight on that airline. But sadly, more often than not, they would corner me to tell me what a horrible flight they had. They would continue to say how an agent or flight attendant did them wrong or was rude to them. And then I'd have to listen to them rant until I could untangle their hold and excuse myself. So after being cornered several times too many, I decided to say, "I work in a big metal tube". That is true most of the time. I guess it sounded so boring and people would just say "Oh" and walk away. Mission accomplished.

Flight attendants were known to have little buzz words that they said when they meant something else. When a customer really irritated a flight attendant, and they really wanted to say, "screw you", or worse, they would say "I'll be right back." And never come back.

There were also rules and regulations written or implied. You do not hang around the podium where the customer service agents are working.

This is true for paying passengers, but really true for employees. The easiest way to get your name accidentally "dropped" off of the standby list, is to bug them. They had so many things they needed to do when starting out and closing out a flight. You just needed to check in with them and then sit down and wait patiently. But do sit close enough by so that you can hear them if they call your name. No matter how tired or low energy you were, when your name was called, you popped out of your seat like a champagne cork. Nowadays, it is all automated so you can see where you stand (am I second or third in line, or am I number one in seniority?) When you walk up to the boarding area today, the screen is shown in the gate area for all to see. You can see how many people wish to be upgraded and how many of those seats are available. It would also show how many people had already checked in. I would cringe when I saw employees or their eligibles hanging around the podium waiting to see what was happening next. And to make sure the customer service agent knew they were there waiting to get their names called. In desperation, I once saw a customer service agent, when someone would not budge from their spot on the side of the podium, pick up the microphone and say the following: "Ladies and gentlemen, as I am trying to close out this flight, I would appreciate our customers having a seat in the boarding area, so I can do my job properly." I think the employee/eligible got the message and everyone else heard it too. Can you imagine trying to work with someone's hot breath on your neck and looking over your shoulder?

Then there was that old joke about the pompous passenger who was demanding to be upgraded to First Class and arguing with the customer service agent. "Do you know who I am?" he bellowed. With that, the customer service agent picked up the microphone and spoke to everyone in the gate area, "There is a man here who doesn't know who he is. Can someone who knows him help him out?"

One day I was traveling on a business trip for the airline. That is a positive space ticket, so when I checked in, I was given a "real" seat assignment and a boarding priority number. And on this particular day, I would be seated in First Class! Of course, there are those very rare occasions when you might be asked to give up your seat. But again, that was very rare on a positive space business ticket. A business ticket indicates that you have a meeting to go to and you have to get there. There I am, waiting for the boarding of my flight, minding my own business, when I ran into an acquaintance. I can only describe him as a "used car salesman" type. Not to be too unkind, but he was pretty pushy. He came over and wanted to see where I was sitting. I was trying to be vague so as not to gloat, but he wouldn't take silence for an answer. "Let's sit together" he says (hoping to be up in the First Class cabin with me). "I'll go get the agent to re-seat me and get me upgraded to sit with you," he said as he jumped out of his seat. "Noooooooo," I pleaded. As he rushed the podium, I didn't have time to tell him that I (as an employee) could not bug the customer service agent and he shouldn't either. So there he was talking it up to the agent, who was getting annoyed with him, and me, I'm sure. I'm back there in the waiting area cringing. Then he sat down and the agent called my name. "Ms. Newlin?" she said. I ran up to the podium, ready to apologize. She said, "I reassigned you so that you could sit with your friend." "Here's an Economy seat" (waaaaaaay in the back). Well, that didn't work well for either of us, did it, Mr. used car salesman?

*   *   *   *   *

I RECALL THAT I WAS 34 YEARS YOUNG. I was on an airline softball team. That is how I chose my team number -- 34. We played co-ed softball on our own time when I was working in the Turbine Shop. Then we all decided to form two airline teams (men and women) to compete with other airlines. Since we were a San Francisco-based team, we named our ladies' team "The Alcatraz Slammers," because of, well, Alcatraz. We had t-shirts made up with a jail cell on the front of the shirt, and our file numbers below. File numbers were given to every airline employee when they were hired. That number stays with you your entire life. I still use that number as a retiree, when needed. Then we had our personal numbers in real big letters on the back. Mine, as I have mentioned, was No. 34.

One day, I was at bat on our newly formed team, and someone was winding up to pitch to me. I put my hand up to say "time out" and we stopped. I said to the pitcher, "Did you go to St. Theresa's Catholic school in first grade?" She said yes. I remember you! We were six years old, and I recognized her from our class picture. She looked the same, only grown up and now 34. We remain friends now to this day, but we hadn't seen each for almost thirty years before that day.

Our group of different airline softball teams were known as NASA (National Airline Softball Association). On passes, we would fly out to a destination on a weekend for a tournament. Bill accompanied me as did the significant others of a bunch of couples. He'd pack his cleats and his glove, should one of the teams be short one person on our men's team or even other airlines' teams. It was all great fun. Delta had a group of accounting people who called themselves the Delta Debits. Southwest had a great group and they all wore stylish uniforms. The Pittsburg group had uniforms just like the Pittsburg Pirates and so on. We had official rules and official umpires, who we fondly referred to as "blue." We played teams until we were all eliminated, and one team was left. That was the winning team. Sometimes if we were eliminated early in the weekend, we would just stand by for a flight home earlier than planned. Or we stayed and cheered on the other teams. Bill and I would usually leave earlier if we were eliminated, since that gave two more employees a better chance to get on the flight. That was better than if we waited for everyone to stand by as a team. Oh, what games we played.

Now, there is an issue with an entire softball team flying standby. You never knew who was going to get on the airplane, if anyone did. Some would be boarded, and others would run to check the next flight out to the same destination or to a destination nearby. Somehow, we made it many, many times. We played often in Phoenix, sometimes in Minneapolis, and many other areas that we could easily fly to.

A few of us rented cars once we reached our destination and all chipped in for the car rental. On one occasion, one of our players got a low-rider Cadillac El Dorado pimp mobile. She was a scream driving it around town. We rented a similar long "boat" of a car and drove up alongside them. She and her passengers slid down in their seats like cool dudes and so did we. We were laughing so hard. I'm sure it was not unlike distracted driving.

This same player made up silly limericks that we used as cheers to root on our team. We all sang the songs at games. I still remember every single word of the limericks, but today they are not politically correct.

One time in Phoenix, we were playing so well, that we were not getting eliminated. It was getting late Sunday night and we were still in the mix. Most of us had checked out of our rooms that Sunday mid-day. Bill and I, for some reason, held onto our room for another night, planning to cancel it once we were eliminated. Well, we won the tournament! We had the big trophy. It was late Sunday night, and none of us could return home on the last flight from Phoenix to San Francisco. It had already departed. Our only choice was to stand by for the first flight Monday morning, getting us into San Francisco around 8:00 a.m. Most of us started work at 8:00 a.m., so we knew we were going to all be a little late. It did, however, look like there were empty seats on the Monday morning flight. But where will everyone stay? In Bill and Rebecca's room, of course. We piled about a dozen or more people into our hotel room. We grabbed bed pillows, throw pillows, blankets, and wraps. We slept in our clothes to stay warm and tried to go to sleep. Men, women, and teenagers. Well, we all started giggling, and then laughing, so we didn't get much sleep that night. We're not entirely sure why but the cops came. Maybe we were a little too loud and someone called them. Our softball coach answered the door and was standing next to his then thirteen year old daughter. The officer looked at the coach, then at the girl, and then at all of the people sleeping everywhere. He asked what the heck was going on in there. We remained church-like quiet while coach Bob explained the entire situation. I guess we all looked like otherwise decent folks, because the officer just told us to pipe down and go to sleep. After he left, that got us snickering yet again. It was really funny at the time. Then we started doing the bit that the Three Stooges did – snore, whistle, and say "me, me, me, me". We stayed awake for several more hours. And yes, we all made the first flight to San Francisco the following morning, again looking and feeling our very best. We were in the same clothes we had on the day before and what we had slept in. We took turns showing our bosses the trophy and we said how proud the airline should be. We were trying to defend our reason for being slightly late for work. I don't think anyone got into trouble for showing up late, but we tried to be more careful at our next tournament. Oh, and did I mention on this particular Monday, I was starting a brand new job at the maintenance base? And my new boss actually understood, thank goodness.

In that same tournament, I was at bat (and batting was not my strongest suit) and somehow I batted the softball into the outfield. Bases were loaded. I ran to first base not very fast, (as my husband fondly tells me) but more like I had a piano on my back. Running fast was also not my strong suit. I was a great catcher, however. The coach waved me on to second base as I was "skylarking" wondering what the heck was going on. And so on, I ran, until I came home. A grand slam! My first and only. I'll never forget that! What a thrill. I couldn't believe it!

The airline teams would sometime play softball in warm, lovely conditions. Other times, we'd be wearing black plastic garbage bags over our heads with the top cut out (like a poncho) because it was pouring rain. It was just so darn much fun. It was also pretty hard to look presentable afterwards when standing by for a flight, because we were representing the airline. But look presentable, we did, sort of.

So. San Francisco

*　*　*　*　*

THERE WAS A TIME (HARD TO BELIEVE) WHEN THERE WAS NO SUCH THING AS A CELL PHONE. When they first came out, they were rather large and bulky. Then they became smaller. Now some are large again, but much more lightweight. But when they first arrived on the scene, it was a real status symbol to own your own cellphone. Only the crème-de-la-crème owned one. That must have meant that they were frightfully expensive when they first came out. I walked gate to gate on my daily rounds of visiting the flight attendants and assisting them if there were issues in pre-departure duties. I remember one man dressed in a fancy business suit with his attaché at his side and his cell phone up to his ear. He was (what appeared to be) talking on his phone to "someone" and having a big, important conversation. While it was still up to his ear, it rang! Busted. He wasn't talking to anyone. He was pretend-talking to look big and important. Status symbol indeed! Now it is so commonplace. I sometimes wonder if he still does that just to keep people from talking to him, much like people put on headphones on airplanes, so their seat mate won't talk to them. And yes, I've done that myself, or even feigned that I was taking a nap.

Once I was approached to be an actor for an in-flight video. Wow, sure, I'd love to. Those selected were told to show up around midnight for an all night photo shoot. We were to wear business attire. I wore a gray suit, with a nice blouse, stockings and heels. They said they would have a makeup artist there to put on TV/video worthy makeup. Well, this lady made us up like "glamour shots" (you can look washed out on camera with every day makeup). We all walked around looking like hookers in business suits. We laughed at one another, yet we tried to stay professional. Even the guys were made up. Even though the inflight videos were just a few minutes long, many of you in the "biz" know that shooting a few minutes of anything, can, and did, take all night. We moved around and the director gave directions to move to this seat and stand over there, and so on. I was given a seat and told to "not" look over the seat top, but just show a little of the top of my head so it looked like there was a passenger in the seat. While the cameras were rolling, I sat up really straight so more of me could be seen. I even arched my already too high eyebrows. It was like the "Kilroy was here" posters. The top of my head, my forehead, my eyebrows and part of my eyes were in full view. "Cut," yelled the Director. Oh well, I tried. We were in the maintenance operations hangar with no one but the actors, directors, workers, lighting people and audio people. After all was said and done, I was in the video. Well, my hands and arms were. I was the person sitting in an airplane seat, who was placing the suitcase under the seat in front of me, while the voiceover said to do so. I could see part of my business suit and my hands and arms. I made sure to show my wedding ring. It was, however, the real deal and very exciting. We worked from midnight to 6:00 am. "It's a wrap," we were told. So we left to all go home and get some sleep. Unfortunately, I had to stop at a store before going home, and I forgot about how much makeup I had on. I could see people looking at me oddly and I only realized it when I walked into our home and looked in the mirror. The pancake makeup was caked on and while yes, I was in a business suit, I did look like a "lady of the night" who also had had no sleep!

I guess I did a decent job of acting, because someone else asked me to be the voice for a retirement audiograph. An audiograph? What is that? I was put in a soundproof booth in the Maintenance Training department. I had headphones and I was to read the written word I had in front of me. Although, without it sounding like I was reading it. I thought I did pretty well. What I didn't know is that if you are reading the text at the end of the workday, and you leave it to continue the following day, you may not sound the same in the morning as you sounded the afternoon before. So you have to work on getting the right tone and energy in your voice. The guys in the booth heard it and coached me, just getting the right sound. Audiographs were a now-old-fashioned recording device that gave you a "tape" you could take home to review before retirement or take it for questions after you retired. It was a question and answer dialogue with a man and a woman (me) discussing tips on retirement. We were both supposed to make it lively and interesting. Afterwards, I was called back to do something even more mischievous. The vice president was retiring and they wanted to do a little something unique for *his* retirement audiograph. He was going to have it presented to him at his retirement party. A portion of it was going to be played for him and the partygoers. So I went back into the booth, and they fast forwarded to one particular section where a man asked me a question. My reply on the original recording was an energetic "Why, yes!" For the vice president's recording only, my response was "You bet your sweet ass." Ha ha. It was funny, and don't let anyone tell you that engineers are boring. They were all a pretty great group. I sometimes wonder where those relics of audiographs have gone. I will bet there is still one around somewhere. There's always an office "saver" (or hoarder) somewhere. We all have one of those co-workers.

*   *   *   *   *

A BLESSED PERK OF WORKING AT THE AIRLINES IS THAT WE HAD ENOUGH MONEY WITH BILL'S JOB AND MINE, THAT WE COULD AFFORD TO TAKE UP THE SPORT OF CAR RACING. We raced cars for thirty years and we both instructed new drivers for almost twenty years. We raced on racetracks in California and Portland, and in the Midwest, among other places. We did not have children, so we wouldn't be putting money away for colleges or weddings. That was our rationale for attempting this expensive sport. After almost thirty years of this amazing adrenalin rush, we were contacted by our club's headquarters on the East Coast. They were looking for two driving instructors to fly out to Santiago, Chile to teach some wealthy Chileans how to drive their beautiful cars (mostly Porsches and a few Ferraris) on a pristine racetrack at speed. We were honored to have been thought of as the people who could do it. We called the gentleman in Santiago. He mentioned that he could arrange our flight and we told him that we were airline employees/eligibles. We could fly standby and just show up. Fantastic. Then he asked us if we could bring another couple to assist us. Well, at the time we had companion passes (buddy passes, we sometimes called them) and we invited another racing couple. Our flight was glorious. It was a 777 and we got International First Class. We enjoyed a lovely Chilean wine, a marvelous steak dinner, a movie and some napping in some luxurious leather seats. We were on our way to South America. The only glitch was while napping I guess I was having a little nightmare. The lights were low and the cabin was quiet…and I awoke suddenly screaming. The flight attendants rushed out, the passengers were abruptly and rudely awakened, and I was so embarrassed. I whispered to the flight attendant, "I'm so sorry, I think I was having a nightmare." Geez Louise. P. S. Louise really is my middle name.

We met such lovely people in South America, some of whom we stayed in touch with for a few years. One person was Gabriel, who we are still in contact with and who has visited us in California a few times. The Chileans were so very cosmopolitan and Santiago was beautiful. There

52

appeared to be only two classes of people – the extravagantly rich and unfortunately, the desperately poor. It was the year 2000 and it appeared that every single person had a cell phone held up to their ears. I noticed it right away when we arrived. The fresh produce there was the biggest produce I had ever seen. The Chilean diet is Mediterranean – lots of sea bass, vegetables, and good wines. The racetrack was new, clean and tidy. We took turns driving their cars and showing them the correct line to drive. Then we rode as passengers to encourage good habits and to discourage bad habits. One gentleman handed me the keys to his brand-new Porsche with almost zero miles on it, and he asked me to drive him around the track. (This is not a dream – it really happened). I put several miles on his new car before he did. They had towed it to the track in an enclosed trailer. Most everyone did. The track was out of the city area, and the road was a little rough. They did not want rock dings on their wonderful cars. I can't blame them for that. They all had a blast, and so did we. We would break for lunch and they would have this lavish spread of food and the wine was flowing. Uh, hey folks, you can't be drinking and driving. In California, that would have never happened. Certainly not at the racetracks we frequented. The closest thing to that would be when we finished racing for the day (when the last racecar had been given the checkered flag), you could hear the "pop, pop, pop" of the beer cans being opened. The Chileans provided us our lodgings so it really wasn't a super expensive trip. And we fell in love with Chile. It's a good thing because the following year, we were asked back. They asked us to bring two more couples. So we went again with two employees/eligibles and four companions.

One of our instructors, a woman, was also a teacher. In true teacher form, she asked the young son of one of the Chilean drivers why he wasn't in school? The boy told her that his parents had taken him out of school for the day so that he could come with them to the racetrack. She asked him in between driver instruction, which subjects he was studying. Then she took the time to help him with his homework. I thought that we had invited just the right person to come along with us on a companion pass.

There are pros and cons about traveling with companions, but these companions were great and we had some marvelous trips.

We had three women and three men instructors. We were three married couples who all raced together in California. We noticed all of the men were driving but no women. We asked them about that. "Oh no", they said. "Here, the men drive and the women take the pictures." We thought, but it's the year 2000. So we three women talked to the women and told them that they should try driving and that they would probably enjoy it immensely. And then the male instructors, well, actually Bill, told the guys that if you want to buy expensive parts for your cars, you would more likely get the wife's buy in, if she is your co-driver. He started something! We took a large handful of women out to learn driving at speed, and we even had some awards for the "first time ever female drivers."

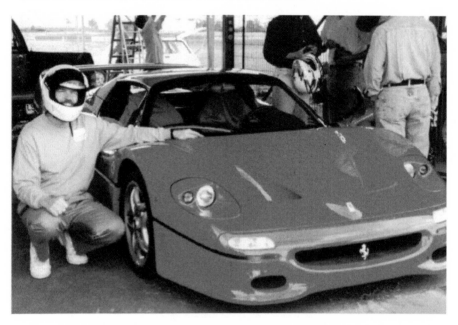

Instructor Bill in Chile

When I turned fifty years old, for my birthday present, Bill got me a ride in a NASCAR mini truck race at Altamont Speedway. In order to drive a truck in that race, I had to apply for and receive my one and only

NASCAR license. I was as happy as a clam giving truck racing a try. A lot of friends showed up to cheer me on and also another fellow driver/friend. I got into an already beat up truck. There were no rear view mirrors on these trucks. I guess they had been long since sheared off and never replaced. I had to turn my helmeted head around a lot to see who was around me, or who was passing me. We had an inverted grid/start. That means that the two new drivers in that race are placed in the one and two positions to give us a head start. The race started and there were the two of us in the front. But not for long. These were seasoned mini truck racers. We passed some drivers and we got passed a lot. We drove the wheels off of those trucks and it was a real hoot. Towards the end of the race there was a guy in the front position, with the guy in second place gunning for him, very close by. I got "t-boned" by another truck, which pushed me into the first place guy. I pushed him off of the track with my truck, and the second place guy went on to win the race. The winner of the race actually came up to me after the race to say "Thank you, ma'am".

Oh it was blast. But I had signed a form that said if I damaged the already beat up truck, I was liable for the amount of the damages. And yes, I hurt the truck a little. Once the race was over, I waited and waited to get the bill. I picked up my mail one day a few weeks after the race and there was my bill – for eighty-seven dollars. That's it! Whew. I dodged a bullet on that one. I still have my expired Nascar license in my possession just for nostalgic reasons.

Happy Rebecca in her NASCAR truck race.

* * * * *

OUR AIRLINE HAD AN ALMOST ANNUAL FRIENDSHIP FAIR. They had airplanes out on the tarmac for people to walk through and look at the latest, greatest new aircraft. They had clowns and games for the kiddies and soda and hot dogs for days. It was just a real down home kid-friendly fair. There was a lot to see and do. There were food kiosks and had just what you would find at a fair. Employees would supervise the lines of people who waited to board the aircraft and we had greeters at the doors of the airplane. We just had good crowd control. It was either free or a very nominal fee to go to this fair. Parking was ample but there seemed to be thousands of people milling around. Everyone would have to park very far away. They also had a car display, as there were so many employees that were into racecars, or dragsters, or just show cars. The people who showed their cars were let in free. You drove your car up onto the tarmac to stage the cars all together. You just hung out by your car and let everyone look around and you just answered questions. We put our racecar in this car show.

Driving on the concrete instead of asphalt was a very different experience. Asphalt is forgiving. Concrete is tough on tires because it has to be strong enough to land an airplane. But that experience helped us when we went to Crow's Landing in California for a car race. It was once an airport with the widest, hardest concrete runways that were a thrill to drive on, but brutal on tires. We would take our oldest race tires, drive the tread right out of them, and just leave them there in the dumpster. We towed our racecar on a single axle trailer. A regular racetrack usually had more narrow roads to race on so you always had the discipline of staying on track and not dropping a wheel in the dirt. At Crow's Landing, however, you drove flat out and took a corner without lifting off the gas. If you did spin the car out, you just spun out on the concrete. Rarely could you even run off the track because there was so much concrete track on the runway. Talk about a confidence booster!

Speaking of racing, we were racing cars while I was still working at the Maintenance Operations Center. Somehow, I was contacted by someone to run a story of a "female" racecar driver, as there weren't many of us doing that at the time. Of course, I was thrilled. They brought out photographers to the Sears Point Raceway (now Infineon Raceway) in Napa, California. I wore a set of mechanic's overalls and I had my helmet under my arm like the real deal. It was very rewarding, and they published the pictures along with a very nice write up in our company wide newspaper (in those days, typed and printed). What I didn't know was that in Chicago, Illinois, there was another female employee who did nearly the same type of racecar driving that I did. They ran a second article about her along with pictures, in the very same newspaper issue. It was really fun to know that we had something in common even though we didn't know one another.

At Infineon Raceway, the former Sears Point Raceway

We were still racing cars when I was nearing the end of my career with the airlines. There comes a point where you have to make an economic decision in order to retire. After all you will no longer get a nice fat paycheck every two weeks. When we realized this, we decided to wind down the sport, and it was at a very appropriate time. I just said to myself, "now is the time," at least for me. I fully expected to still accompany my husband to the race track if he was not yet ready to call it quits on the race-track. Fortunately, about three weeks after my decision, Bill declared, "Yep, I'm ready to call it quits on racing, too." So we did and never looked back. It was a wonderful expensive hobby, and we left while we were still on top. And thirty years is a long time! Having said that, we still have gone to some indoor kart places just to drive the karts and enjoy a little adrenaline rush! In fact, at the last place Bill worked before retiring, the employees loved go-kart racing. The company would throw their annual Christmas party at the local go-kart track nearby. We did this for maybe three years, but the employees started to get tired of Bill and I always coming in First and Second. I wonder if they still go karting without us?

*　*　*　*　*

WE TOOK A MARVELOUS EUROPEAN TRIP WHICH INCLUDED A
STOPOVER IN MONACO. It was gorgeous. Besides seeing the changing
of the guards in the palace, we got to go into the casinos and watch the

high rollers gambling. They were wearing tuxedos and sipping martinis – shaken, not stirred. Just like in the James Bond movies. It was such a wealthy place and we were enthralled. The yachts in the harbor were spectacular and while we were there, the weather was stunningly beautiful. We would walk along the harbor and stare at the wealthy people lounging on their spectacular yachts and we could've sworn we overheard them asking the question, "Do you have any Grey Poupon?" Oh no, wait. That was us when six of us rented a houseboat on the delta years ago and would call that out when we were passing a big boat. And we'd laugh and laugh, and they'd look at us with such distain. And of most importance to us as racing aficionados, the Formula One race is held there annually on the Monaco streets. We had longed to actually see a Formula One race in Monaco but it is frightfully expensive. Instead, we watched it on television. We happened to be on a tour bus with another couple of our racing buddies. We talked the bus driver into driving the track with the bus. The race is held on the streets of Monaco, so it was fairly easy to do. Going through the famous tunnel gave us such a good feeling, even if we were on a bus and we might have been going forty miles an hour. It still was a thrill.

On this same trip, we managed to get to Italy and saw and climbed the Leaning Tower of Pisa. We were able to go up the stairs and walk around the tower. However, it was very unsettling because the gates in front of us were only about knee height for us tall folks. I'm fairly certain the gate height has been raised. If not, there would be a lot more casualties.

Bill at the Leaning Tower of Pisa.

We also did the tourist thing in Venice, Italy and took gondola rides with our friends. And yes, we did sing, "O Solo Mio". And yes, the sailors wore the striped shirts and hats and were so very nice.

*   *   *   *   *

FINALLY WE DID GET TO SEE OUR ONE AND ONLY FORMULA ONE RACE IN PERSON – IN MONTREAL, CANADA. We flew standby and worked our way through cities to get to Canada. Once there we stayed at a lovely Bed and Breakfast – there were six of us! The other four flew out on paid tickets. Each day of the practice, qualifying, and actual race, we would step out with our backpacks. We would walk to the underground train, stopping first at a local deli to pick up sandwiches and sodas to pop into our backpacks, and get on the underground train. They have their own world underground with restaurants, hotels, stores, trains, etc. We rode to a certain stop and when we got out at ground level, we were right there at the race track. What a thrill. This was a one-time only for us (bucket list), but we never miss a race on television. This way we can adjust the volume. We all had to wear noise diffusing headphones, it was THAT loud! I actually got teary-eyed when I spotted those drivers that I followed so closely on television, driving right in front of us. You could almost see their faces through their helmets. It was wonderful. We did some research to see where the Red Bull team and the Ferrari team were staying and walked into that hotel after the race to have lunch. We saw Christian Horner, Red Bull Racing, and others. My friend and I were going to the ladies' room and we walked right by that very handsome Mark Webber, a Formula One driver at the time. To drive a Formula One racecar, you cannot be too large of a person. I would guess that a driver cannot be over 5'10" and no more than 150 pounds to fit in those racecars.

It was a marvelous trip. We went out to fine dinners in the old part of the city, complete with cobblestone streets. As we were leaving, they were tearing down all of the racing items and setting up for a jazz festival. Oh, how we wanted to stay for the jazz festival. Technically we could have, since we were retired and were flying standby. But we didn't stick around, unfortunately.

The other two couples had paid for their tickets so we parted ways at the airport terminal and off they went. The Montreal airport is really lovely. I happened to notice a nice, new hotel right smack dab in the middle of the airport. A glass escalator rode up to the hotel nearby the gate areas. I looked up there and thought how nice it would be to stay there some time. Well that wish came true rather quickly! We were not able to get on the last flight of the day out towards San Francisco. They could accommodate us the following morning, however. There appeared to be open seats for the next day. So we took the glass escalator up to the hotel and asked for a room for the night. They had a room and what a nice room it was! It was on the Executive Level. We were right on time as happy hour was going on. There were drinks and food in a large conference area with big screen televisions, and anything else you could want. Well, that was enough for a complimentary dinner. Yes, the hotel was not planned, so it wasn't in our budget. But we rolled with it and had a lovely time. The best part of the next day was having a shower in the morning, drinking coffee, having a little breakfast nosh, and just stepping onto the glass "down" escalator, right near our gate. We got on the flight the following morning.

*   *   *   *   *

W E HAD A MARVELOUS TRIP TO GERMANY ON ANOTHER OCCA- SION. We again were traveling with another couple. While Bill and I enjoy traveling with another couple, we also really love to travel with just the two us. We are on our own getting to and from our destination anyway. On this trip, however, the four of us rented a car at Frankfurt airport. We got in our car and drove around and around the airport for more than a half an hour trying to get out of the airport. The signs were so confusing! We would see the word "Ausfahrt" which we thought meant exit, but it was in fact an exit that was meant to be passed by vehicles, like a parking garage. Exits which were meant to be passed by pedestrians were called "Ausgang". Because we didn't know, we circled around and around. We finally made it out onto the autobahn. Now the four of us were racecar drivers, but when on a regular road, we liked to follow the rules and stay somewhat within the speed limit. Besides, our companion was a California Highway Patrol- man. But there didn't seem to be any speed limit that we could see. We had this little four cylinder car that was shaking and rattling and going as fast as its little cylinders could make it go. Suddenly we saw and felt a Mercedes Benz blow by us at twice our speed. Whoa! This was our first experience on the autobahn.

In 1989, I WAS WORKING IN THE PERSONNEL DEPARTMENT, AS A PERSONNEL REPRESENTATIVE. It was just about quitting time for the day, when a big earthquake struck! I've been through several earthquakes in my life. I am a native San Franciscan and we lived on the San Andreas Fault. The room this day was swaying, and my boss and I dove under our desks. I remember watching the baseboards moving up and down like they were made out of rubber. But the most unusual thing happened with the file cabinet. There was a four-drawer, tall file cabinet nearby and we had a couple of VHS's (you know, the old-fashioned video tapes) on top of the cabinet, just sitting there. When the shaking finally stopped, the VHS tapes were all under the file cabinet. They had fallen off of the moving cabinet. The cabinet had apparently danced around a little and came to rest on top of the tapes. You just never know what will happen during an earthquake.

At the airport terminal itself, I saw the devastation the following day. It looked a little worse than it really was, as the overhead tiles had fallen out in many places. There were exposed wires and internal stuff hanging out of the ceiling. There was also dust and debris made by falling tiles. It was just a dusty mess. We made our way home that previous evening to check on our home. The lady across the street displayed lots of tchotchkes on several shelves, and most of them were all over the floor. Right across the street, we entered our own home only to find one picture that needed to be straightened. No cracks anywhere! We were so relieved.

* * * * *

WE ALWAYS DID HAVE A GOOD TIME IN THE OFFICE. I recall when I worked in Personnel with a female boss and two other male co-workers. We worked hard but we could laugh while we were doing it. One time my boss and I were talking "girl-talk." (You know, about shoes, stockings, dresses, and such.) The boys yelled over, "Talk about boy things and airline-related stuff". So I yelled back, "The Boeing 767 is powered with a Pratt & Whitney JT9D-7R4A engine." We all cracked up as one of them said, "That's what

I'm talking about." I guess I remembered it from my old Turbine Shop days and didn't even realize I had that in my mental arsenal!

Now, this isn't a smart move, but I once stayed late to interview mechanics for employability. My technical counterpart was not available, so I interviewed some people on my own in a deserted office. My plan was to rate them as suitable for employment or not. Then I would forward those good candidates to my technical counterpart, who would then review their resumes for suitability as an aircraft mechanic. One of the questions we had to verbally ask, even though it was on the application, was "Have you ever been convicted of a felony?" This was to assure us that the question was indeed asked. We would initial it to show that it had been also verbally asked. I'm alone in the office with a male candidate and I ask that question. Even though the interviewee had written "no" on the application, when I asked him, he said "yes." Gulp! "And what was it for?" I meekly asked. "I shot and killed a man!" Gulp again. And? "He was in bed with my wife." Oh wow. I diplomatically finished up the interview nervously, I'm certain. I thanked him for his time and ushered him out to the lobby where a guard let him out of the building. Thankfully, that was the last interview for the evening, so I closed up shop immediately. I really was frightened and my knees were trembling. I decided that day that there would always be some-one with me in the office at all times when working late. Even our beloved security guards weren't close enough to me to help me if I needed help.

Another time I was interviewing a very nervous young man. I was trying to get him to settle his nerves, so I asked him about some of his hobbies. He said one of his hobbies was "gynecology." What? He said, "you know, the study of precious stones." Oh *geminology* you mean. "Oh sorry, I thought that was what I said." Actually, the word geminology means the study of twins. Gemology is the study of precious gemstone materials. Now I can understand why he might have been confused.

* * * * *

W<small>E</small> EMPLOYEES/ELIGIBLES DRESS DIFFERENTLY THAN MOST CUSTOMERS WHO TRAVEL WITH PAID TICKETS. We dress nicer, that's all. In the old days more customers did dress up, but that has changed over the years. Paying customers tend to dress more comfortably and casual. But we were the ones wearing suits, or sports coats, ties, nice shoes, dresses, etc. At the Maintenance Operations Center, there was a lovely janitor who cleaned our restrooms. She was such a marvelous lady that we would talk whenever we ran across one another. I always noticed that she cleaned the sinks with the most beautifully manicured hands with a bright finger polish color. She also wore lots of sparkly bracelets. She was so classy. Then one day I saw the lady janitor in the boarding area standing by for the same flight as we were. Oh my goodness! She had on a gorgeous fur coat in those days when it was a super-popular thing to do. She was really decked out. I figured that she was paid very well (after all, it was a Union job and there was a negotiated pay scale). Either that, or she was just wealthy. I was very proud of her in any event.

* * * * *

W<small>HEN</small> BILL AND I WERE FIRST MARRIED, WE LIVED IN A ONE-BED-ROOM APARTMENT IN BELMONT, CALIFORNIA. It wasn't bad, but we had some sketchy apartment neighbors. But the apartment rent was only 140 dollars per month. I was working more of a nine to five job at the airlines so Bill and I could commute together. We loved going to the mailbox where more often than not, a gift check would be waiting for us. A lot of Bill's relatives lived far away from us and would send us wedding checks. They just kept coming for several weeks after our wedding. Around that same time, we had our getaway car that we drove to our honeymoon place in Carmel, California. It was a 1963 Austin Healey convertible. We sold it to another apartment neighbor on a Friday night. We took it off of our insurance right away. The new owners were going to put the car on their insurance the following Monday. Well, it got stolen on Saturday night, right in the carport. I felt so bad for the new owners. I know it was not yet insured, so I don't know what they did. Hopefully, there was a loophole they used to either find their car or worked something out with an insurance broker.

Some time later, some Hell's Angels moved in. They parked their car next to ours in the carport and their Mustang had a bullet hole right through the front window and through the front seat! The Hell's Angels were a couple. They had lots of friends coming over all of the time and at all hours of the day or night. They were rather loud too, with big booming voices. Our bathroom cabinets were back to back. If I opened my cabinet at the same time they opened theirs, it would be like we were in the same room. I could even see some daylight through a slat. While we couldn't see them (thank goodness), we could really hear them.

About eight months into our marriage, Bill got his orders to be deployed on a West-Pacific Navy boat trip aboard the U.S.S. Decatur. It was during the Vietnam era. Thankfully he was on a ship in Vietnam waters and didn't have to set foot on Vietnam soil. He was deployed to many wonderful places, including New Zealand, Australia, Hong Kong, and American Samoa. At one point he let me know that he was going to be in Hong Kong. He would be there for a couple of weeks. I decided to take my vacation days and fly on a pass to Hong Kong. I had been working days and just marooning on my apartment island by nights. I'd have my minute steak and salad dinner almost every night. I did some sewing and just basically stayed in. It was a nice sanctuary and I felt safe enough, even with some interesting characters living next door. So I packed and packed for the trip. I had new outfits that I made myself and shoes to match each outfit. I had a lot of luggage. This cured me. I had to lug around so much luggage, that I vowed from here on out to pack one bag only. I figured if I really needed something, I'd either do without it or I'd buy it. We still pack this way.

When our airplane left San Francisco, there were no medical issues going on in Hong Kong. In the several hours of flying to Hong Kong, there was an outbreak of smallpox. By the time we landed, all of us passengers were ushered into a medical room. We were lined up and given our vaccination -- right there in the airport. Only then could we join our families and depart the airport. The shots were done at no cost to us and were greatly appreciated.

I joined Bill and a dozen sailors for dinner that night in downtown Hong Kong. I remember it was a pretty fancy Chinese restaurant, very ornate. There were fish tanks all around the dining area. Whenever someone ordered a special kind of fish, a chef would reach into the tank and grab the requested fish with his bare hands. Talk about fresh!

There was lots to do in Hong Kong. It was very cosmopolitan and appeared to be very wealthy at the time. The shops were fancy and there was so much to see and buy. I had a list as long as my arm with me from friends and family. They wanted me to buy things for them. Cameras, watches, jade jewelry, silk material, you name it. As a marked contrast, in the water were sampans -- boats where people lived, slept, and worked aboard. They were mostly fisherman, but as you watched them go by, you could see that their entire family was likely on board. There were also trams that seemed to go way up to the sky and what a great view there was from up there. It was a very good trip and of course a delight to be reunited with Bill for a couple of weeks.

Once I had to go to Hong Kong on business, not pleasure. The airline put me up in a very swanky hotel indeed. It was huge room several floors up in a high-rise building. It had a full honor bar and snacks. I got a beverage and something that looked like Pringles, some chips in a cylinder container and started munching. Eeeeewww! They were dried fish chips. So back I went to the honor bar in search of something salty. When I went to bed that night in a huge king-sized bed, I had a remote control that moved the blinds up and down. I lowered them for the night, right from my bed. It was so cool. Then in the morning, before my meeting, I got up and made a pot of tea and jumped back into bed (I still do this to this day – it's my ritual). I got my remote control and raised the blinds. Blinking a couple of times, I quickly lowered them again. There was a guy on some scaffolding on my floor washing the windows. So that's how they clean windows on high rise buildings. That job would not be for me!

*　*　*　*　*

Have you ever heard the term "slam-click"? This was probably coined by a flight attendant. Now there are at least two kinds of flight attendants. The first one is the kind of person who likes to drop off his or her bag in the hotel room, and hit the streets running. They like to go to restaurants or shopping. Then the second kind of person is the sort who goes into his or her room, slams the door and clicks that bar on the door to secure it. This is usually when a flight attendant has been to the same location many times and has seen everything there is to see. They might just want to sip tea, read a good book, and take a bubble bath. I've been that sort of person from time to time. I was frequently observing flights to Japan and after awhile, I became a slam clicker. I would read or watch television. The Japanese cartoons were silly and fun. The "bad" guys always had round eyes! And then one time I was watching CNN because it was in English. They did a segment on the Pumpkin Weigh Off in Half Moon Bay, California. All the way from Japan! I was watching it with interest and suddenly see my hubby, Bill, right in the center of the frame. He was watching the guys weighing these enormous gourds. It almost made me cry, I was so happy to see him. Now this is not too much of a coincidence because Bill knows how to work it. He gets on television often by standing in just the right place at the right time, when cameras are rolling. But it was very exciting, and of course, I became homesick.

We took a trip to Frankfurt, Germany one time, and ended up going to other places in Europe as well. We were on our own, so we were going there with absolutely no plans to speak of. We just wanted to tour museums, take trains, and see things we hadn't seen before. We loved the train station. And when they said a train will depart at 10:00 a.m., at 10:00 a.m. it was moving out of the station. They were extremely on time. People had to be on the train minutes before the departure time. The train station itself was so lively. It was fun just to hang around in the train area. We walked around, ate hot dogs, drank warm beer, and just people watched one afternoon. We saw this customer with a cute doggie in his arms, asking for a train ticket and how much it cost. After being told the cost, he pointed to his pup and asked, "und schnauzer?" He wanted to know how much for the pup. It was so cute.

Later on in that same trip, we worked our way to the Black Forest. It was so lovely and lush. And then we found our way to the Porsche Factory and Museum in Stuttgart, Germany. At the time we had a nice gently used Porsche 912 (it was a 1968 coupe). It wasn't too expensive at the time. We were curious about how they made them, so we worked our way over to Stuttgart. Everything then was done by hand, no robots to be found anywhere. With no reservations for the factory tour, we walked up to the front of the factory door. "Is there a tour here today?" we asked. "Yes," they said. "There's one in a half hour." Great, we thought. Then they informed us that the tour guide would be speaking Spanish. Well, neither one of us was fluent in Spanish, but we wanted to take the tour anyway, just to see the goings on. We sat on the curb outside the factory waiting for the tour to start. We saw Porsche after Porsche drive by us, driven by a factory driver. They were testing out the cars. What a dream job! What a great car show we had from our curbside spectator seating.

The tour started and the guide introduced himself and asked where we all lived. Once we told him we were from California, he spoke in Spanish to all of the Spaniards and spoke English to us. This was clearly doubling his workload. But we really appreciated it. We saw all the inner workings of the factory and all of the car mechanics. Everything was tidy and very clean and the process was so precise. When a whistle blew, the mechanics immediately stopped what they were doing, and started taking their breaks. Just like clockwork of course. We walked by the soda machines like the ones we were accustomed to seeing in the United States. But instead of sodas, there were beers. They could take a beer break during the day. Ah,

Europe. Europe was far more casual than the United States in that regard. While in Switzerland, near some relatives' home, we once saw roofers up on someone's roof fixing the tiles, with a glass of vino in one hand. What would OHSHA say?

From our days in the Porsche club and attending car conventions over the years, we had befriended a lovely lady who worked at the Porsche head offices. As we didn't know if or when we would get to Germany, we did not give her a heads up about our being nearby. We thought we would just call her up. We did, and she was available. "You should have let me know in advance," she said. But she still took time out of her busy schedule to take us up to their private lunch room and we three had lunch together. She said she could not even imagine traveling without reservations or without having all of her ducks in order. We mentioned that we traveled "seat of the pants" but that had little meaning to this well-organized German lady.

* * * * *

My last job at the maintenance operations center was fun for the first 21 years, and then it got to be a burden. I was working a few hours at home before work, working a ten-hour day, and then being asked to work on my weekends off. I would get up at 4:00 a.m. and turn the light on in the walk in closet of our home, so as not to disturb Bill. I would lay all of my paperwork on the carpeted floor, sit on the carpet, and organize it for my crazy day ahead. I was at my wit's end and way overworked. When I could no longer see a solution, I sent a desperate letter to my boss. I told her how overwhelmed I was. Then I asked her if I could transfer to another job somewhere, anywhere. This was at a time when we had maybe one huge computer for the entire office and we had to put our name on the computer with a post-it note when we needed to use it. So you can imagine that it was difficult getting anything done and done in a timely manner. And I was being asked to do tasks that I simply did not know how to do.

A vice president asked my boss one afternoon for a spreadsheet containing certain statistics. My boss asked me to do it and have it ready for the vice president by the end of the day. What? We had just gotten that one computer and most of us only knew how to type on them. This was unlike the kids of today who grew up with computers as infants. A spreadsheet? How in the world? I went to some computer people in another department for answers and instructions, but it was still Greek to me. It broke my heart that I could not complete this task by day's end. I was overwhelmed and I pleaded with my boss. I just did not know how to do it. I had never been trained to do a spreadsheet. She understood, thankfully and helped me get an interview with Onboard Services as an inflight supervisor. Had she not been able to accommodate me, I had briefly considered leaving the company. Looking back, what a mistake that would have been. But that's how desperate I was. Onboard Service was a godsend. It's where I spent my last fourteen years before I retired. Wow, what a ride!

I was then in my 40s and to be a credible supervisor of flight attendants, I went to flight attendant training at our hub in Chicago, Illinois with all the other twenty-something new hires wanting to be flight attendants. It was fun and challenging.

3

MY LIFE AS A FLIGHT ATTENDANT SUPERVISOR

Now, flight attendants are some of the most interesting people i have ever worked with in my opinion. There was seldom a dull moment. They told me some of the best stories about what went on in the air during a flight. One of them once told me, "… you should hear the stories we *don't* tell you."

One of the many tales the flight attendants told me was about "the honeymoon couple." They came onboard together and were cooing and hugging one another in their airplane seats near the front of the cabin. Then they drank too much. The brand-spanking-new hubby passed out. The new blushing bride got up and walked down the aisle. The next thing you know, the flight attendants spotted her canoodling with a perfect stranger and they had a blanket over them. Goodness knows what was going on. Duh! The flight attendants were quietly chatting about it in the galleys, but they had to get back to work as the plane was nearing landing. The bride heard the fasten seat belt sign, realized where she was, and walked back to her original seat, where her unsuspecting husband was still sleeping it off. He woke up, the plane hit the runway, came to a stop, and the newlywed couple walked out hand in hand. Okay, so I wonder what stories the flight attendants are not telling us!

What I learned from flight attendants is that what they give out as their personality and kindness, they get back from our customers. If someone came back from a full flight and dropped by to tell me they just had a glorious flight, I usually could tell that they had been kind to our customers. And thus the customers were kind to them. The flight attendants usually received some commendations from customers. It's not that hard to be kind. Oh, and vice versa. "That was the most horrible flight with some of the most horrible people," some would say. Hmmm. I wonder what sort of mood that flight attendant was in when he or she served our customers. We had a saying that was basically "pack two bags – take one with you and leave your other baggage at home." It made sense to me.

Some of my best-performing flight attendants did amazing things for our customers. While working in First Class, one flight attendant was asked for a hot mocha latte by a customer. We usually have only coffee on board. Instead of her saying "Sorry, we don't have that," she said "let me see what I can do." She poured hot coffee in a mug, dropped in a Godiva chocolate and let it melt. She put in some whipped cream and stirred it all up. Then she topped it off with more whipped cream. The customer was delighted. How creative, huh? It might have only have taken two or three extra minutes to make our customers happy, maybe less. Well worth it in the long run.

Another First Class customer asked a flight attendant for a Bloody Mary. This flight attendant told me he always traveled with a bottle of Worcestershire sauce and a bottle of Tabasco. This was in the good ol' days when you could bring liquids onboard through security. He would make a killer Bloody Mary that everyone seemed to love. Customers often told us that the flight attendant went the extra mile to make sure they had a good flight. They did this by completing a comment card that was made available to our customers.

As a supervisor, I sometimes got to work a flight just to work alongside our flight attendants. I'd do this maybe one to two times a year. Once, when I was working the bar cart with another flight attendant in the Economy Class, a customer asked for some ice tea. "Sure," I said. The flight attendant working the bar cart with me quickly said, "We don't have ice tea, we just have hot tea." I said, "I'll make it work." We had a saying that the customer is not always right, but the customer is always our customer. If we can go an extra step for our customer to make his or her flight more enjoyable, why not give it a try? I know when I do something nice for someone, it makes me feel better.

It was so easy. I just poured some hot tea over a glass of ice cubes and let it melt, added more tea, and more ice, and a small wedge of lemon, and voila! Iced tea. She kind of glared at me like I had done something wrong, when in fact, I had done something right. She might have been one of those flight attendants who came home from a trip and told one of us supervisors, "That was the worst flight ever! With the worst supervisor, ever."

Speaking of supervisors, we all had nicknames. There was the "dragon lady", "the witch", etc. I asked one of my flight attendants what my nickname was. I had a very good rapport with her. "I don't think you have one," she said. "What? I want a nickname!" So she thought about it for a moment and said, "Well, you are a tall person, so how about Amazon bitch?" "That'll do," I said, giggling. It got shortened to AB, which was fine with me. I'm also AB to my nieces and nephews. They call me AB, short for Aunt Becky – or *is* it?

On another trip, I was working again as a flight attendant in Economy Class. I was working the bar cart and doing a pretty decent job of it. I was diving in to the ice cubes with the scooper, scooping ice in a glass – when I got carried away. I flung the ice cubes wildly. The ice landed on a sleeping female customer with ample cleavage, dead center on her breasts. Without thinking, my instinct was to put out my hand and retrieve the ice cube. But I knew I couldn't do that as she might wake up and see my hand coming towards her, and misunderstand what I was going to do. Can you say lawsuit? So I didn't do anything. I kept walking by her seeing the ice cube slowly, very slowly, melting on her.

On another trip, I worked as a flight attendant yet again. Now remember, I work one to two times a year, and I'm not very adept at it. It's a skill that takes practice. We just didn't get enough practice. On this particular flight, I was assigned to work the First Class cabin (Gulp!) So I read up on all the rules and service flow charts. I saw that there was a certain way to go through the cabin to offer a post-departure beverage and include a heated ramekin of mixed nuts prior to the meal service. I was fine with the pre-departure offer of a beverage. I took the order for a gentleman in Seat 1A. I fixed the drink but forgot to bring the drink out along with the ramekin. So I placed the drink on his tray table and realized I had forgotten to bring the ramekin. I ran back to the First Class galley to get it. Now the Purser, seeing that the customer in 1A had a drink and no ramekin, quickly placed the ramekin onto his tray table. So I walked out of the galley with a ramekin and got to the gentleman. Now the tray table is resting low on his lap, near his crotch area. I looked down at his tray table and blurted out, "Oh, I see you have nuts!" What? I ran away into the galley and stayed there until my faced stopped burning and the redness went away. I was so embarrassed and there was nowhere to go. And he just smiled at me. So, for the rest of the flight, I paid attention to all of our customers but particularly to the customer in 1A, trying to make up for my gaffe. Imagine my surprise when some weeks later my manager showed me a commendation card that had been filled out saying what a nice job I had done in First Class – from the gentleman in 1A!

I think people take for granted what the flight attendants do. It's an effort to get passengers settled for a flight (and sometimes some people just won't sit down). They have to do a pre-departure service, then a post-departure drink service (with nuts). Then the attendants offer a meal service, followed by a snack service if the flight is long enough. Finally, they have to pack everything up and check seat belts for landing. And of course ensure the customers' safety throughout the flight. That's the number one priority. Then there are those international flights where the flight attendants also brought around Duty Free items in case the customers wished to purchase a bottle of spirits, or an Hermes scarf, and other items. Oh, you know there are many more duties our flight attendants provided, but some of them were behind the scenes. They included counting meals, assuring we have what we are supposed to have boarded on our airplane.

It's the little things that work or don't work. I was in the back galley getting the coffee pot to serve the front customers in the Economy Class. I picked up the coffee pot with my right hand and a serving tray in my left hand. I walked through the aisle to the front of the cabin. Once there, I realized that I couldn't pour coffee with my right hand – I just couldn't. I'm left handed. What to do? Walk all the way back to the aft galley and change hands? Instead, I casually set the pot on the tray table of the customer in the front of the cabin and changed hands. It was probably not the classiest way to do it but I had to make it work.

＊　＊　＊　＊　＊

ON SOME BUSINESS TRIPS TO CHICAGO, WE WERE ASKED TO ATTEND THE IN-FLIGHT DINING CLASSES. Yes, that's right! What a dream for a foodie like myself. The classes consisted of a presentation of a new type of service, possibly with a new Chef. Everything had to be tasted and tried to see if it was worth the cost of changing up the menu and switching to another Chef.

We had to try the latest champagne. Check. It's great. We had to sample the Godiva chocolates. Check. They're great. How about the new hors d'oeuvres for the First Class cabin? Bring it on! And so on. Of course we discussed the service flow. Service flow is whether to serve our customers from the front of the cabin to the back of the cabin, serve from the back to the front of the cabin, or start in the middle and end up at the forward and aft galleys. Service was done in many ways. We chose what was best for that particular flight on that particular aircraft. Flight attendants were always included in the service flow discussion. That part was great but the tasting was da bomb! I got to meet Chef Jacques Pepin. We were all given his cookbook and he signed my copy. We had two other Chefs who were All-American, but they specialized in Mexican food. They had a couple of restaurants in the Los Angeles area at the time. Our airline had hired them to make dishes we could serve on our airplanes. Food was very fancy at one time and then that era changed.

Pardon me for saying this, but we always tried to accommodate our customers by having a number of fish, chicken, or beef dishes on hand. But what's with customers getting angry at our airline when we ran out of say, chicken? The caterers could not possibly know how many people wanted beef, or chicken, or fish, or who were vegetarian. If they boarded 200 meals for the Economy Class, how could we possibly have known that maybe 200 customers would show up wanting fish. We just received a ratio based on a guess or previous statistics – 100 people might want beef, 50 people might want chicken and another 50 people might want fish. It was so non-scientific.

One customer from India was onboard. He ordered a specific vegetarian dish and when the flight attendant presented it to him, she inadvertently gave him a chicken dish. He realized it immediately, waved his hand around wildly to signal to her to remove the dish. He then put his hands together as if in a prayer position, and said, "Nooooo, I am vegetable." She realized what he wanted, and clarified that he wished to have a vegetarian dish instead. But he just kept saying over and over, "Noooooo, I am vegetable".

In International First Class, which is even better than Domestic First Class, we offered such a fine service. Among other things, we might have Dom Perignon and/or Johnny Walker Blue. That was my first time seeing Johnny Walker Blue. At the time, I had a friend who was very into his scotches, particularly the Johnny Walker types. There was the red, the black, the gold, the green, and maybe more. Each one seemed to cost a little more. When I was looking at a special gift for him, I found a bottle of Johnny Walker "Swing". Since I had never heard of it, I figured he might not have heard of it either. He hadn't. So I bought the Johnny Walker Swing. What I didn't know was that the glass bottle was fashioned in such a way that the bottle rocked, or swung, hence the name Swing. So when he took it out of the gorgeous gift box, he set it on the counter and it rocked! Before I knew it, I had lunged over to where it was rocking to catch it before it crashed to the floor. He laughed and said, "Geez, it must have been an expensive bottle of Scotch for you to immediately react that way." It was! So when I was working on a flight, I went to the First Class cabin to see how the service was going and to see the latest offerings. There was a bottle of Johnny Walker Blue. It was in a stunning blue box lined with white satin, which, frankly, reminded me of a classy casket or coffin. But it was so lovely, and the passengers told me how good it was. "I'll have to try it some sometime," I said. And I did, when I wasn't on duty, of course. And I enjoyed it. I told my scotch aficionado about Johnny Walker Blue and he said, "There's no such thing." Oh yes, there is! I saw it with my own eyes. He researched it and there it was. It started a fun thing among our scotch-drinking friends. Bill and I bought the Johnny Walker Red (the basic and least expensive) and painted the bottle blue with glass paint. Then we would (and yes, this is tacky) cross out the word "red", and write in the word "blue" with a black Sharpie. Oh, how our friends got a kick out of that. One guy told me he kept the blue painted bottle. He just kept refilling it with Johnny Walker Red. You really do learn a lot of things onboard the aircraft that you can use out in the real world, some seriously important stuff!

* * * * *

At one time, the flight attendants, pilots, supervisors, and managers, shared the upper deck of the airport, alongside the crew schedulers. The crew schedulers made up the trip pairings for flight attendants and pilots. That was fun, because all of us were interacting and we did not have separate offices or separate areas. The running joke was that pilots were very frugal. They enjoyed huge salaries as they should, however. They are piloting our planes after all. But they were still well-known as being very careful with their money. Either a flight attendant or a crew scheduler glued a bright shiny penny on the floor nearest the pilot crew area. We watched with glee as the highly paid pilots reached down to pick up the penny on a daily basis. The penny never budged from the floor and they sheepishly walked on, hoping no one saw them. Hey, a penny saved is a penny earned, right?

Speaking of the crew schedulers, they were the backbone of the trips that the flight attendants took. They figured out the pairings of trips and the legal hours to fly them. The flight attendants were mostly nice to the crew schedulers in the hopes of getting the very best trips to fly. When flight attendants got a horrible trip that they really didn't want, they would secretly, okay, maybe not-so- secretly, call the schedulers, "screw schedulers." But mostly they all got along.

Remember those placards in the airplane lavatories (blue rooms, as we called them) that said something like "please clean up after yourselves?" Actually, it was much more diplomatic than that, but flight attendants were always cleaning up the lavatories and they expected that passengers would do that as well. I always did. I would clean up the paper towels on the floor, and mop up the sink and leave it better than the way I entered it, even as a passenger. It's something I just couldn't seem to unlearn.

* * * * *

W E WERE STANDING BY ONE DAY, FOR FLIGHT AFTER FIGHT TO TRY TO GET SOMEWHERE NEAR WHERE BILL'S RELATIVES WERE HAVING A FAMILY REUNION. We told them in advance that we would be there if we could get on a trip with a pass. We were sitting with a good friend and his partner and the four of us waited and waited, trip after trip. This friend HAD to get to his destination because he was speaking at his niece's wedding the very next day. After several flights, we decided we would call it a day. We would explain to our family by telephone that we could not get on a flight. Our friends, on the other hand, walked over to another airline and plunked down a wad of money and bought two full fare tickets. They got on the very next flight to their destination. Last minute ticket purchases can cost a pretty penny. But different priorities called for different solutions.

When we were more immature (in our 20's), we would pass the hours waiting for a flight by going to the white courtesy telephone where you would pick up the receiver on the wall phone. An operator would answer and you could page anyone right in the airport on the loudspeaker. You'd hang up and a few moments later, the "voice" would say something like, "Paging Mr. Ben Dover" or Dr. Seymour Butts, or something even more sophomoric. And we'd laugh and laugh and then run up to the white courtesy telephone and do it all over again.

We were told early on by some senior employees that standby's should stay put in the gate area even when you are told there is no more room on the airplane and the gateway bridge was closed by the Customer Service Agent. We sat there until the plane backed away from the jetway. Why, you might ask? Anything can happen and often does. Someone may have been on the airplane trying to locate their seat and got a call right there and then that their meeting was cancelled and they didn't have to go on the flight after all. This had happened to us a few times over the years. The door would fly open and a couple of passengers deplaned. If we were there ready to run down the jetway at warp speed, we'd get their seats. I noticed that a lot of employees bolted from the gate the minute they heard the flight was full. They were looking for another flight to sit and stand by. They apparently didn't know our secret.

Once, we were stuck in Denver on a holiday weekend (4th of July). I was always near the top of the list based on seniority, but this particular time Bill and I were maybe numbers twenty-two and twenty-three on the list. A flight or two would become full and the customer service agent would close out the flight. All of the pass riders left the boarding area. Not so fast! We stayed at the gate waiting for the plane to back away from the jetway. The agent somehow did a headcount on board and found two more open seats. The agent ran out to the boarding area and started calling names in order. No one answered because most standby's were gone -- until they got to our names. We were right there waiting, and got on the plane, chanting in our minds "close the door, close the door."

Also as SA's, we traveled light. A purse for me, a wallet for Bill. We always checked one small bag each. That's it! In the 35 years I've worked for the airlines, and the over 14 years of being a retiree, we've only lost our checked luggage two or three times. It was always recovered in a few days. We packed our oldest clothes so that if we ever were to lose them, they were not our "Sunday Best." We would not mind if they were lost forever. Besides, without carry-on luggage you could really run through the airport to get from gate to gate.

I can remember sitting at a particular gate where there were two seats open. We happened to know that Bill and I were number two and three on the standby list. A pilot's wife was number one. If she took the number one seat, I might be offered the other one and that would leave no seat for Bill. Rarely did we split up on a trip. Yes, sometimes there was a First Class seat for one of us (we took turns) and an Economy seat for the other one. We would split up for the flight but we'd still be on the same aircraft. So there we were, waiting to hear who was being called onboard. The agent walked over to the pilot's wife. She was there with massive amounts of large luggage. "Is that all for you?" the gate agent asked, pointing to the luggage. The pilot's wife nodded. Then the agent looked at us with our one purse and one wallet. She said "quickly, come with me, you're on the flight." Again, we ran down the jetway elated. However, I did feel bad leaving the pilot's wife behind.

As standby's, we were told never to ask a paying customer to change a seat for us so we could sit together. You just sat in whatever seat you were assigned to. Sometimes, however, customers would see us walk on together and then split up to sit in seats opposite one another. Invariably someone would ask us if we wanted to sit together. "Oh no, that's okay. Thank you." But if they insisted on moving so that we could sit together, we would do it so as not to disrupt things too much as we needed to get settled quickly. Of course wearing a corsage on my lapel helped out as they thought we were newlyweds. That last sentence I made up. But someone did tell me that it worked for them!

Occasionally the flight attendants knew me and I would be in the Economy Class, sitting next to a full-fare customer. The flight attendant might whisper to me, "Can I get you a hot cup of coffee in a china cup and saucer, and maybe a cookie from First Class?" I would whisper and thank them and say yes if they could bring one for my seatmate. This way it wouldn't be too awkward.

We were asked to be discreet about being a pass rider once onboard the airplane because we just paid zero dollars for our ticket (pass). The person next to us might have paid hundreds of dollars. If someone said something like "you must be a million miler or an important customer because everyone seems to know you," I would just smile and say thank you. However, every once in a while, someone would grill me. They would ask things like where do you work, what do you do, do you fly often, where do you travel? It was at that point that my book would come out or I'd put headphones on or turn on my in-seat television. Always with a smile of course.

*   *   *   *   *

A FRIEND RECENTLY SHARED WITH ME WHAT HER PARENTS DID IN THE GOOD OL' DAYS OF AIRLINE TRAVEL AND JUST HANGING OUT AT THE AIRPORT. She writes:

"My parents often took a few hours a week to have their own vacation, their time away from home, but in an unorthodox way. Everything with my parents was unorthodox. From the earliest age I remember my mother and father driving out to the San Jose Airport, not to watch planes take off and land, but to sit in the lobby for hours and watch people board and de-board planes. San Jose airport was not yet the San Jose International Airport. It was a fraction of its current size and much more friendly. It was easy to get from Point A to Point B. Now you need a detailed map application on your phone to get from one end of that airport to the other, or to find your parked automobile, or locate the car rental building. But I digress."

"Watching complete strangers walk off planes and greet their friends or relatives was my parents' homegrown entertainment. They'd watch the hugs, the tears, the heartfelt greetings with great interest. Then they would go out for drinks. In the 1960's, San Jose Airport was like its own reality show."

In the "glory days" going to the airport was like an open door policy. It was super easy in those days (the 60s) to go in and out of security. It was like walking into any place of business. Someone looked at you, smiled, and then let you in. That changed as time passed. As an employee, I had to go through security every day to get to work. By the early 90s, some of us knew how to bypass security by going underground. It was like an amusement park down there. You would see the conveyor belts with the carts of luggage in them criss-crossing like a roller coaster, up and down, across the room, turning corners, coming and going. I was fascinated by it.

While going underground to get to work one day, I noticed that the elastic on my half slip under my suit skirt had given way. (It does that after years of laundering it.) My gait was impeded by my slip sliding down. So I decided to duck into a room to quickly hike up my skirt and pull my slip up. I knew that I would take it completely off when I got to the office. I didn't want to worry about my half slip all day -- I had a job to do! So I proceeded to hike up my skirt in what I thought was an empty room. I then realized that I was in the ramp servicemen's break room and it was break time. Oh my goodness! I ran the rest of the way to my office hoping that no one in the break room recognized me. And, no hearty applause. Nothing.

Then on another day I was walking behind one of my co-workers, trying to catch up to her. She had something stuck to the back of her suit above her waist. As I got closer I could see it was some material clinging to the fabric of her suit. Static cling! It was a pair of unmentionables. She had no idea. I told her about it and we laughed and laughed and we were both glad we were in the underground area – the bowels of the airport, so to speak.

*   *   *   *   *

SOMETIMES, IF SOMEONE HAD, SAY, A TWO- OR THREE-HOUR LAYOVER IN SAN FRANCISCO, ENROUTE TO ANOTHER DESTINATION, THEY WOULD CALL US AT HOME. We would drive right over and have breakfast or lunch with them. And just hang out with them until they were ready to leave for their next segment. That was a fun way to catch up with an out of towner. With my badge, we could breeze right through security and meet up with friends. Even now, as retirees, or even employees, you must have a ticket (or pass voucher) to get through security.

Security had been tight, then more relaxed, then tight again. One of the things one had to do on occasion was get patted down. I went through the metal detector and if it beeped, I got patted down. So some woman came over and started the process. (Or if you are a guy, a man will come over and pat you down.) I must have gone through security thousands of times in my life. Shoes off, shoes on. Belt off, change taken out of your pockets. And I had a titanium rod in my right leg from a surgery – knee to ankle. I always set off the alarms. But the TSA's got to know me and understood. But I do feel satisfied that, for the most part, they tried to make us all safer.

I had a really funny co-worker who would go out of the security area for breaks and lunch. I wondered why he would go through the trouble of walking outside of security, knowing that he would have to go back through security multiple times a day. He simply said, "I like getting patted down." Okay, then.

*   *   *   *   *

AIRPORTS ARE RADICALLY DIFFERENT FROM ONE ANOTHER. Take a big international airport in San Francisco. San Francisco airport has moving sidewalks, gallery exhibits, shops, restaurants, and cocktail lounges. It also has long jetways to assist in enplaning and deplaning passengers on and off of the aircraft. We had one occasion to travel to Toledo, Ohio. I don't know what I was expecting in an airport, but I wasn't prepared with how simple their airport was in those days. We'd pull up to the "gate", which was really a gate, a cyclone fence. A small staircase on wheels came up to the aircraft door and we were all ready to walk out of the airplane. However, it was raining, so there was the gate agent with an umbrella holding it over each passenger as they walked out. It makes me smile to think how even though it was a tiny airport, it functioned as a real airport and it worked for them.

We traveled on a pass to Chico, California one Easter morning to spend the day with my sister and her family. I understood that my sister, her daughter, and her daughter's two kids would be picking us up. Now Chico is a tiny airport as well. We pulled up to the airport gate -- a wall, really. I saw that the airport was deserted almost completely, except for four people standing near the wall. As they came into focus I saw that they were my family – the only ones there that day. The gate agent pushed the moving stairway up to the airplane, ran up the stairs, opened the door, and let us all out. Then he ran to the middle of the plane and was unloading bags from the cart that his co-worker had just driven up to the side of the airplane. Then they drove the baggage carts filled with bags over to the little terminal. While we were getting our bags, he ran over to the departure gate and looked to see if anyone was there to take the next flight out. A real two-man show. When we returned to the airport for the flight back, those same two workers were there. It was almost as if they were the only ones working there ever.

The Las Vegas airport was a lot larger and more flamboyant as you might expect. Several supervisors and good friends all stood by for flights to Las Vegas to stay for the weekend with another retired supervisor for a "Girls' Weekend." I wonder now what the flight attendants thought when a gaggle of supervisors boarded their flight. We told them we were on pleasure travel and not business. Girls just wanna have fun! When we arrived at Las Vegas airport, we heard joyous shrieking in the lobby. I seriously wondered what was going on and then saw a bunch of slot machines right there in the lobby. People were winning money. We heard the "ching ching

ching" of the machines dropping coin after coin. The passengers were going wild. It was wonderfully bizarre. On our trip home, there we were, back in the "casino" that was the Las Vegas airport. We just had to try our hand at the coin machines so we too, could have "slots of fun". Then it was our turn to shriek when we got as little as, say, ten dollars. If you were on stand-by and trying to get out of Las Vegas, (it's very difficult) it was a great way to while away the hours.

* * * * *

Do ALL EMPLOYEES OF A COMPANY PARTY EXCLUSIVELY LIKE WE DID? I occasionally went to dinner parties with our engineers, and maybe a brunch or lunch with my personnel folks. We also had office parties and showers for co-workers. When I got to Onboard Service and started working with flight attendants, only then did the invites start pouring in to backyard parties and pool parties. Even the supervisors had parties. Pool parties with flight attendants were a blast. It was always just a good time with swimming, eating, drinking, games, dancing, singing, last minute made up fashion shows, you name it. Generally these folks were far from shy. I remember one very gregarious fellow at a party. He donned his swim trunks and a long pink boa and walked around the poolside as if he was walking a runway.

* * * * *

ONCE I AND A DEAR FRIEND AND CO-WORKER DECIDED TO FLY IN TO SAN FRANCISCO, AND WE CARPOOLED TO A RESTAURANT FOR LUNCH WITH OTHERS. I had accidentally left my lipstick at home that morning. Seriously, who leaves on a trip without lipstick? I didn't realize it until after I had wiped all of my lipstick off with a napkin after having a cup of coffee on board the aircraft. I couldn't see my co-workers without lipstick! I just couldn't. They drove me to a drugstore in Millbrae and I ran in and bought a lipstick. Then we drove to the restaurant. Saved by the lipstick!

Oh, and that reminds me of the time I checked into my hotel room after a long flight and got ready for bed. I had just taken off all of my makeup. When every trace of makeup was removed, I realized with horror that I hadn't brought ANY of my makeup on this trip. Yes, I'm a little vain but I knew that there was a little store downstairs in the lobby. I could probably purchase something for the next day. But in order to do so, I had to have some makeup on to walk down there to buy makeup! The next morning, I looked around. I found a No. 2 lead pencil and put on my eyebrows. Done. Then I took the lead and made some shadow to put on my eyes. What about lipstick and blusher? I just pinched my cheeks until they were pinker and went downstairs without lipstick. Just for a couple of minutes. I bought way over-priced cosmetics in that little store but I didn't care at this point. I went back upstairs to apply it properly. Dodged a bullet on that one!

* * * * *

THEN THERE WERE THE LEAN DAYS OF THE AIRLINE. Management employees who were on business trips had to share a room with another person or persons at our Chicago office/hotel. Some were dormitory-style rooms with up to four beds. There was only one bathroom. Now, flight attendants were union employees. Their contract stipulated that they would have their very own rooms, lucky them. So one time I got to the hotel and walked in and locked the door. There were four beds and I only needed one. But I wasn't sure if I would be sharing my bedroom with others or who these people would be. I got ready for bed, went to sleep, and some time later, I heard a click of a key in the door. A beam of light appeared as someone (another employee, I'm hoping) comes into the room. This person gets ready for bed and finally turns off the light. I fell back asleep. When my alarm went off in the morning, I woke up and noticed that the unmade bed was empty and I was again alone in the room. I got dressed and went to my business meeting all the while wondering who the person was. Was it a man or a woman? I'll never know.

* * * * *

ONE OF MY BEST FLIGHT ATTENDANTS WAS RETIRING AND SHE WAS GOING TO BE WORKING HER LAST OFFICIAL FLIGHT ONE DAY. She was in complete uniform and had a great big corsage pinned onto it. We called her CB. Those were her initials and CB just fit her. She was previously married to an airline captain and they had a daughter. Now their daughter was a twenty-something gal with blonde hair and blue eyes and she looked like a teenager. She was, however, an airline pilot. It was a family affair with the airlines. So on CB's last flight, we had cake and festivities and CB went to the gate to work her last flight. The captain was her ex-husband, and the first officer was her daughter. She got on board and soon the passengers were seated. The captain made an announcement, "Good morning, ladies and gentlemen, this is your captain speaking. Onboard today is a special flight attendant. We used to be married. She is working her last flight before retirement. Please wish her congratulations and help make her last flight memorable." She was met in the cabin with cheers and applause. Then another announcement came over the loudspeaker. "Good morning, ladies and gentlemen, this is your first officer. The flight attendant retiring after this flight today is my mom. Her name is CB. It also stands for call button. If you want to wish her well or if you need anything at all, please contact CB by pushing your call button! Often! Yes, it was a memorable flight, I'm certain.

If we travel somewhere with just the two of us, we like to be adventurous. We'll pack for Maui, as an example, and we might end up in New York City. Often if we were traveling on a pass, there might not be any seats to that location. So we would run to the list of boarding aircraft and see what other flight was leaving shortly to try for that flight. The O'Hare Chicago airport is a wonderful place to do just that. If we were trying to get home we ran up to the board, looking for any of a number of flights leaving shortly, and ran to the gate. We'd try for Denver, Utah, Las Vegas, and then San Francisco, Los Angeles, San Diego, or anything heading west. We'd eventually get home. We always have. Maybe it takes a day or more, but eventually we get home. Of course, that doesn't work as well when you are with other folks, particularly friends with a store-bought ticket.

One weekend we were in Oceanside, California for the weekend. We had flown into John Wayne Airport and had rented a car. That was on a Friday, and that gave us until Sunday morning to try to get home. That would be pretty much two full days. We made the most of those two days as we always do. So on Sunday morning, we got to John Wayne Airport in Orange County and turned in our rental car. We started standing by for every flight to San Francisco. We were getting a little antsy about mid-day, as we both had to be at our respective jobs by 8:00 a.m. the next morning and Bill had an important meeting he could not miss. We were still sitting there around 8:00 p.m. on Sunday night. Well, that was the last flight for the evening and we didn't get on. The next flight was the next day, Monday morning. It was not only a sold out flight, it wouldn't arrive until after Bill's meeting started. What were we going to do? We went back to the rental car place and re-rented the very same car we had rented on Friday and had turned in on Sunday. We started driving home. Orange County to San Francisco -- about seven hours. We arrived in the wee hours and tried to get some sleep, a shower, and make it to work on time. Monday night we were exhausted, but we did it!

A very senior flight attendant told me this story when she was working the First Class Cabin in the early 60s. In those days, the Monday morning business traveler was almost exclusively male. That particular day it also happened to be the morning of Halloween. The flight attendants wanted to dress up for the customers just to start their work-week with a smile. "But what shall we dress up as?" they thought. Wives! That's the answer. Their thinking was that many men had just jostled their sleeping wives out of a deep sleep to give them a kiss before leaving on their business trips. Could they find an easy bunch of inexpensive costumes? Yes, they could. So after take off, they quickly donned slippers, bathrobes, put plastic curlers in their hair and cold cream on their faces. They walked through the aisle offering coffee, tea, and breakfast. One passenger was overheard saying "I just left that at home." It sounded like a grand idea and probably was a lot of laughs.

Once we stood by for several flights from SFO (San Francisco) to LAX (Los Angeles). When the last flight of the day backed away from the jetway we started to leave to go home. We heard the agent say on the microphone, "Party of two, Newlin." We ran back to the gate. They said that there was a plane leaving in two minutes to Reno if we wanted to get on. We ran on the plane to get somewhere, anywhere. Then we thought to ourselves, and just why are we going to Reno? Oh yes. This flight was going to Reno with a minimum crew and no passengers. It was picking up an entirely new flight crew to route them to LAX for another trip. So we were the only customers (and non-revenue passengers to boot) with the flight crew. We chatted with them the entire less than one-hour trip. No service of course, but we were on our way to somewhere. We stayed onboard, another crew came on and we were ferried to LAX. Again no passengers, just us. It was a genuine adventure. And we didn't have to go home that night just to have to come back the next day to try to get to Los Angeles once again. We arrived in Los Angeles very late, but hey, we were at our destination.

One co-worker friend took it a step further. He would stand by for a flight, say, to Puerto Rico. If he saw that First Class was full, he'd run to another gate, and so on, until he found a First Class cabin with a seat available. After one such trip, I asked him how his flight to Puerto Rico was, and he said, "I went to Paris, France. And I flew International First Class, which was great fun."

* * * * *

WE HAD A DRESS CODE FOR THE PASS RIDERS (EMPLOYEES, RETIREES, ELIGIBLES AND COMPANIONS). You could spot us a mile away, at least that is the way it was in the 70s and 80s. We would wear suits, dresses, ties, nice shoes, etc. Now back in the day, customers also dressed up with suits, ties, and ladies in white gloves. This was in stark contrast to the casualness of the customers in the 70s and 80s. I recall seeing a hippie, albeit a rather rich hippie, sitting in the First Class cabin with his bare feet on the bulkhead (wall). If he had shoes with him at all, I never saw them.

THE SERVICE LEVEL IN FIRST CLASS AND EVEN BUSINESS CLASS USED TO BE AMAZING! It was pretty darn special. Flight attendants would serve sparkling wine or even champagne in First Class, offer caviar and would carve prime rib in the aisles. They offered desserts such as hot fudge sundaes or freshly baked cookies. It was pretty incredible.

On some of the big airplanes (747's, my favorite), there was a lovely console in the downstairs First Class section in the center of the cabin. In our more abundant times, Catering would bring flight attendants fresh flowers and lovely items to dress up the console. It made such a good first impression for our International First Class customers. In the more lean days, costs needed to be slashed and the flowers were taken off the list of "must haves." Our resourceful flight attendants would still decorate the console, sometimes with their own items from home - a set of pearls, some Asian fans, etc. It still looked lovely with little to no cost. I always admired that creativeness and told them so when I observed it.

In the Premium classes, there was a spoon and fork technique that flight attendants used. They would hold the spoon and fork in such a way that you could serve the food like a culinary school chef might do it. It was a very elegant way of serving our customers. SAFT-ing, it was called (spoon and fork technique). I never quite got the hang of it, working only a very few trips as a flight attendant per year. It was very awkward for me, but I admired the flight attendant who "worked it" with grace. At one Christmas party where there were a lot of flight attendants (they sure know how to have a great party), one lovely lady mentioned SAFT-ing. My husband spoke up and said, "I know what that means; spoon and fork technique." "Maybe, but we call it 'some asshole forgot tongs.'" We had a good laugh over that. SAFT-ing at its finest.

And speaking of parties, we got invited to a lot of them, with a lot of flight attendants, and/or supervisors. A flight attendant typically would have a grandiose party, and everyone would come dressed to the 9's. The airline taught them how to prepare things so beautifully on the airplane. It just transferred over to their own parties. One particular Christmas season, we went to someone's home in Diamond Heights in San Francisco. Diamond Heights is a very lovely very expensive area. The view that night was spectacular. This flight attendant had a partner who was a music teacher. So there we were hob nobbing with all these wonderful people, when two people sat down at two (yes, two) concert grand pianos. They were both in the living room placed head to head, with the piano keys in opposite directions. The glorious music started in as they passed out song books from a huge fabric lined basket. Most of us knew the songs of Christmas. And every once in a while someone would sing a solo and the roof would shake. When it was a group sing, I thought the windows would blow out of the house. There was such a big swell of glorious music, mostly by the host's voice students. Speaking of voice students, I was so enthralled with the music students that I started taking voice lessons from him. He taught a number of people and did some wonderful vocal workshops. We all sat in sections of sopranos, altos, tenors, and baritones and did voice and floor exercises. And then we had solos. There was such luxurious sound.

Our music teacher was once in town staying at a lovely Hillsborough home. He invited me there to his friend's home for a voice lesson. Wow! I walked into the house and was finally guided to the piano where our lesson would take place. "It's the very same piano that was featured in the movie, High Society," my music teacher told me. I was in awe. That was maybe my very favorite voice lesson of all time in that home.

And I must mention a friend of mine, who also took voice lessons from our teacher. She still has a voice that is so glorious and so powerful, she seldom needs a microphone. It is rich, it is full, it is wonderful. She sang a song that I never forgot. It was "Fifty Percent". At another vocal intensive workshop, an acquaintance did a solo performance from the rock opera, Jesus Christ Superstar – "Gethsemane". Stunning. I still hear both voices clearly in my mind. You two know who you are.

Then there was the luxurious activity of pouring the champagne for our First Class customers. Ever notice the depression in the bottom of a bottle of champagne? To pour, our instructions were to put your thumb into the depression and hold the bottom of the rest of the bottle with the remaining fingers. Then you would put the other hand behind your back very elegantly. Think "Downton Abbey" servers. Are you kidding me? I tried it and almost dropped the entire bottle of that expensive liquid and that was just at home, rehearsing. I never dared try it on the airplane, even in calm flying. And certainly not with any turbulence present. Truth is, I don't think I ever saw a flight attendant pouring champagne in that manner although it was our serving procedure. Cleanup in the First Class aisle!

Flight attendants could be really funny. Some of the things they said to us (hopefully in jest) were very memorable. Besides SAFT-ing, they would tell us "I can't go to work today, I have PMS – Passengers Make me Sick." Now, dear customers, you know who you are. But it was kind of funny. Another flight attendant told me she had an "I" problem. "Eye problem?" I asked. "No, 'I' can't see me coming in to work today." But they were mostly very dependable. The fact that they could be so open and honest with their supervisors was refreshing. It wasn't always that way, however.

I was sitting in my tiny little cubicle having a sandwich around lunchtime. I had an appointment shortly after lunch to meet a new flight attendant for the very first time. She had just transferred in from another domicile. She arrived early and stood at my cubicle entrance with her hand on her hip, very defiantly and ready to attack. "Hello," I said, "I'm just finishing my lunch, (chewing the rest of my sandwich). Do I have anything on my teeth?" She glared at me and said "No." I introduced myself and she said, "Spare me the rhetoric. You don't want to meet me anymore than I want to meet you. I do my job and don't need a supervisor looking over my shoulder." What could I say, but "Well, so nice to meet you." She then turned on her heel and started to walk off in a huff. As she did, she said to me, as a parting shot, "And yes, you do have something on your teeth." She finally came around weeks later (maybe at a different time of the month) and we got to be much more friendly as time went on. We knew where each other stood.

Around the holidays, our airline would host a Fantasy Flight where an airplane would be decorated for the holidays. It would be staffed by pilots and flight attendants. The boarding gate area would be decorated as if the flight was going to the North Pole. There would be performers there and of course Santa Claus and his many elves. The plane would be filled with children who were underserved or had a "Make a Wish" dream granted. Many of the children had never been on an airplane, let alone "Santa's Sleigh" going to the North Pole. Cookies and beverages would be served. Everyone was on board with the mission – just to make children happy for a short while. The captain would make suitable holiday announcements. They would take off, fly around for awhile, and then land back at the gate. The experience was always a thrill even if you were just a supervisor of onboard services who happened to be working the gates and walked to that particular gate to assist with pre-departure activities.

*　*　*　*　*

SOMETIMES WE WOULD STAND BY FOR RECIPROCAL AIRLINES AND THAT WAS FUN. They would give us benefits on their airlines and we would give their employees benefits on our carrier. The boarding priority would differ between carriers. We were on our way to Kenya for a photographic safari (definitely shooting nothing but pictures). Our route was San Francisco-New York-Germany-Lagos, Nigeria-Nairobi. On the segment from New York to Germany, we had the rare privilege of standing by for an international flight on a German airline. We had paid for a 90% off Economy seat. 90% off! And it was standby. We sat patiently in the boarding area, and it was soon empty. "Should we say something, or just wait?" we said out loud to no one in particular. Just then an agent came out and said, "What are you two still doing here?" "We are waiting for a seat," we said. She continued, "Come with me and hurry, the doors are closing." We ran down the jetway (yet again) and she seated us in International First Class.

INTERNATIONAL FIRST CLASS! It was so luxurious, complete with amenity kits, warm booties, and chilled vodka. And a tea service a few hours after a wonderful dinner. We were so spoiled. We loved every minute of it. The flight attendants were very disciplined, direct, and professional. "You vill take your seats!" But it was a marvelous trip.

As pass-riding customers on our airline, if you got into Business Class or First Class, the flight attendants gave you an amenity kit. You accepted it graciously unless they ran short and a paying passenger was not given one. Then they would ask if you would mind relinquishing your kit for a full-fare passenger. Of course we gladly did it. We would wait until all kits had been passed out before opening our amenity kits just in case that happened. That rarely occurred, however. The kits had sleep masks, toothbrushes, razors, combs, mouthwash, and almost anything you might need on an overnight flight. They are yours to keep so I kept them and used them once in a while. I did have some amenity kits that were never opened or maybe one item was missing. I used them when we had over-night guests at home. I would place an amenity kit on their nightstand in the guest room. They always seemed to appreciate that effort. Now, I keep a zippered bag on a hanger in the guest room closet that has all the amenities one could ask for, just in case our guests forget something. A friend of mine made it for me, since we entertain and travel so much.

Oh, how I wanted to go to Africa. I wanted to see the rare animals that I had only seen in pictures. I looked around and saw there was a seven-to-fourteen day tour of Kenya, a photographic safari. Talking Bill into this trip was difficult at first, because he was worried about all the bugs and our safety around all the wild animals. But I talked him into it. Once we were there, he absolutely loved it. The weather was pretty much like San Francisco weather during Indian Summer (September/October) sunny and not too warm.

We met our guide in Nairobi. We were going to be in a kind of open air vehicle that seated six people, plus our driver. What joy. But before we started that part of the tour, we were led to a cool underground type of hotel/barracks. There were single rooms and there were dormitory type rooms. We all had call buttons above our beds like on the aircraft. The buttons would light up and sound when/if a rare animal showed up. Before we went to bed, we sat around this big underground room. We stayed fairly quiet so as not to scare off the animals. We had windows we could look out at ground level and see the animals roaming around. Later, we were in our jammies and asleep in bed when the button lit up. We all ran to our respective windows to see an animal, the likes of which we had never seen. I can't recall the name of the animal but it was rare. Okay, maybe it wasn't so rare, but they made it seem like it was and we played along. I just know I had never seen such an animal. Very interesting. The next place we went to was pretty fancy. It was at a game preserve and we would dine each evening in a fancy dining room. The servers were dressed in white starched uniforms, and it was indoor/outdoor dining. They would alert us when there was an animal in a nearby tree. And they must have had quite a few daily sightings as they had meat secured to a huge branch of a tree to entice the animal to come visit. We must have seen an animal every night we were there, up in that tree.

Our room was very nice, with mosquito netting over our bed. Well I didn't see any mosquitos, but I did see one small lizard climbing up the wall one night. Even though I screamed like a little girl, I was told they were harmless. I scream like a little girl the moment I see any kind of insect or one of God's little creatures. They just scare me. The hotel staff suggested that we lock up our belongings and keep the windows and doors locked when we were out of our rooms. They said the monkeys would come in and mess up all of your belongings, going through them. We never had that happen but maybe it's because we complied with the locking up of the room.

We may have showered and dressed up every night for a swanky dinner but by day, we were dusty and dirty. We drove through the jungle looking at so many beautiful animals. We felt fairly safe, although I was curious that the driver carried a rifle. Yikes. The six passengers got along right away. There were the two of us, another couple who worked at an airline in Alaska, and another couple (a mother and daughter) from an airline based in Texas. In fact, we stayed pen pals with all six of us for several years. For those of you too young to remember, a pen pal is someone you write a letter to in your handwriting, on stationary. You put it in an envelope, and write their address on the front of the envelope. Then you put your return address on the upper left of the envelope, put a stamp on it, and put in a mail box. It gets to them by snail-mail.

The driver rode over bumps and ditches in the road, much to our delight. Wheeeeee! However, while going over one particular bump, a hole got ripped in the gas tank. "Oh no, we're going to be stuck here in the jungle," I wailed. "No," said the driver. "Let's find a gas station." He got a bar of soap from a gas station somewhere and shoved it up into where the tear was, and voila! The hole was plugged for the rest of the day. That night he got it fixed. Who knew soap was good for that?

Since we were at the Shell station I asked if I could use the restroom. I was pointed to the area of the restroom and walked over to it. Where was the door? Oh, it is just a shower curtain, right in public, that you draw closed while you are using it. Where anyone walking by at any given moment could pull back the curtain while you are in there. What? Then I walked in and saw no facilities, just an empty room with a brick missing. So I left and got back into the car. I told the driver that the restroom was inoperative as it had no facilities other than a brick missing in the middle of the room. "No, it's fine. You "go" above the missing brick!" Well, I decided I could wait for a proper bathroom. No thanks!

Then we saw a mama rhino with her baby. Now I never thought of a rhino as being very pretty, but this baby was so cute. Our driver stopped the van to get a closer look. He suggested we step out and go pet the baby rhino. Really? So we gently stepped out and started to walk slowly toward the baby rhino, standing quietly nearby the mama rhino. I noticed the driver had the rifle out and it was aimed at the mama. "What is he going to do?" we thought. He later said it was a precaution in case the mama rhino charged at us because we were petting the baby rhino. Wow, we didn't want any part of that so we all hastily got back into the truck. By the way, the skin of a baby rhino was not unlike petting a concrete wall.

We stopped along the way to look at anything we found interesting. We looked at the Kenya coffee bean plants, and came across a flea market kind of thing, with people and items of interest. There were baskets, ivory-carved animals, weavings, spears, shields, beads, you name it. We heard a lot of Swahili spoken. And then there were the lovely Maasai people. They were good looking people, with flawless dark skin, and white teeth. They were all young. We didn't see any one elderly, at least at the outing. It made me wonder if they lived very long. But these folks were just so carefree, smiling all the time. And tall!

It was a wonderful vacation. We felt safe and well taken care of. The guide thought of everything. And because it was all-inclusive, we didn't have to worry about a thing.

As we were leaving for home, I just had to purchase an authentic spear and shield, which I carried through the airport and took onboard the flight with me to bring home. Why? I wasn't sure yet, but I knew that I just had to have it. Can you imagine bringing a real spear through security these days? No way. But way back then (the 80s), I walked right on board and the flight attendant put it in the First Class closet to hold for me for the duration of the flight. Then we arrived home. What do I do with it?

We decided on decorating our bedroom with an African flair. We painted the walls a beige/brown and then put up bamboo fencing all around the room. We bought Zebra print comforters, pillows and shams. My sister took one plastic half gallon jug that milk comes in, cut it in half, painted it white, and then decorated them with black paint to look like African masks. We put them on the bamboo covered wall. A small plaster zebra graced the foot of our bed on top of a faux bear skin rug. We put the shield on one wall, and the spear standing up in the corner. We thought it looked fabulous and I suppose it did. Today, I wonder what the Property Brothers would think of it!

Some areas we have traveled to have been more beautiful than others. It's always an adventure, but to see some spectacular scenery and beautiful palaces is just a treat for the eyes. We went to the Palace of Versailles. The gardens leading up to the Palace were so grand and we were able to walk around at will. We could see whatever we wanted to see unless it was roped off for some reason. When we stepped inside the Palace, it was like stepping into a glorious movie of olden days. There were powdered wigs, corsets, and lots of lace and satin. Every throne lined up along the walls was covered in jewels and gold. They were remarkable. What was even more remarkable was that we were told by our tour guide that originally those thrones had holes in the seat part and a bedpan underneath. Seriously? Someone was going to be in a meeting so long that they just "went" when they had to right there in front of everyone? I can't imagine but it did put quite the scene in my memory. Now I know why they call toilet seats "thrones."

By contrast, I really didn't care for Taiwan. There was a fragrance of smog and vehicle exhaust, and many people looked so sickly. And even the pets (dogs) looked malnourished. Gee, I sure hope they were pets. It just wasn't that pretty to my eye. I wanted to find something I liked about it. So I went to a MacDonald's while there. They had burgers but instead of fries, they had rice. Not too bad.

Then there was a ferry boat ride out to the White Cliffs of Dover. Imagine blue skies and warm weather and gliding over the rippled small waves. We finally came into contact with Dover. It was a breathtaking sight for sure.

*　*　*　*

For a few years, our airline had a shuttle service where we would pack people into airplanes, as quickly as possible, and serve our customers an abbreviated service. There was maybe just a beverage service and we would quickly get them to their destination in record time. It always made me smile when the boarding and departing music was played. It was very peppy music which they played to get people to jump up, get their bags, and GO! It seemed to work well for many years but it was not a leisurely travel experience. Nor was it intended to be. A year after it was implemented, we had a one-year celebration of our Shuttle service. We had many large sheet cakes in the boarding area along with urns of coffee. We offered them to our customers walking to and from the gates. It was well received by everyone. I had been asked to go down to the gates to assist in this celebration. I was given the task of walking around with a tray of cake slices for our customers. I saw one gentleman sitting alone and walked over to offer him a piece of cake. When he looked up, I immediately recognized that he was indeed Robin Williams. "Excuse me sir, may I offer you some cake?" I managed to whisper. I was in awe seeing this big, make that huge, celebrity. He is very shy when not "on" like he is onstage as a standup comedian or in a film. Rest in peace, Robin.

Then there was the issue of having companion passes for your friends. Some of the pros and cons of companion passes are that if you travel with the person on your companion pass you can be more responsible for their behavior. When you are not accompanying them, you take your chances. I've heard stories about a person on a companion pass hanging around the podium demanding to be put in First Class, and/or not dressed appropriately. So, I seldom used these companion passes. I'm not even sure if I'm entitled to them anymore as a retiree. It's not worth the stress of wondering if your companion will behave in a professional way. Even though we had (mostly) professional friends, you never knew about their kids or their kids' friends.

In 1993, we rode on a pass to Salt Lake City, Utah to go skiing with some friends. The flight was uneventful and the skiing was magnificent. We had some friends living in Park City at the time and they would invite us every year for several years. This particular time, another one of my co-workers was going to join us as we had some mutual friends in common. Now this supervisor/friend was a fabulous skier and skied with her feet together like they were tied with a rope. I envied her style. My style was more like barreling down the hill, close to out of control, and coming to a stop at the bottom of the hill. Then I would run to the ski lift and do it all over again. Knowing my style wasn't pretty, I decided to take my very first-ever lesson -- a lesson in "style." I left the others to do their own thing and I started my ill-fated lesson. At some point, I wasn't even going that fast, but I turned and twisted and my boot didn't go with my turn. My bindings were too tight, I was later told. I came to a stop all twisted. I had broken my leg in five places! The fibula had a break in two places, my tibia was broken in two places. I later found out that I had also cracked my kneecap. The brightest light to all of this (and I can always find a bright spot) were the ski patrol young men who were so attentive and so handsome. There I was, riding in an ambulance all by myself except for the driver and a paramedic and being checked in for an overnight stay in a foreign (to me) hospital. By this time all of my peeps were back at the chalet waiting for me so we could start happy hour. No one believed me when I called them and told them that I had fallen and couldn't get up! And I was in the hospital. And I had broken bones. Finally they showed up and then they believed me. I had a plaster cast all the way up to my groin (or at least it seemed that way). The doctors told me to get home and contact an orthopedic surgeon to have surgery to fix it correctly. I was wheeled to the airplane in a wheelchair. The flight attendants made room for me in First Class (score!) because I needed the room to stretch out. I had an aisle seat and I just extended my leg throughout most of the flight, making sure I didn't trip the flight attendants. They don't like that. And when I arrived in San Francisco, my dear co-workers had a wheelchair waiting for me to take me to our car in the parking lot.

Within a few days of being home, I found a marvelous surgeon at Stanford and went in to meet him. I was surrounded in the waiting room with very tall basketball players and broad-shouldered football players. Some were with the Warriors team and some were with the 49ers. My doc was into sports medicine and he was gorgeous! He was also a new surgeon of about one and one-half years. He actually got excited when he saw my X-rays from Utah. He said something like "how cool," and left the office to show some of his cohorts. The plaster cast was SO TIGHT by this time, that he had to split the cast in half like an oyster shell and wrap it up again (looser now) with a two inch gap between the top and the bottom of the cast. He said I was losing feeling in my pretty blue toes. What a relief that was! I was scheduled for surgery the very next day. The doctor did an epidural and it was not enough to keep me sedated, he later told me. They went to the full anesthesia. The morning after the surgery the surgeon visited me in the hospital and brought me a hot mocha latte. How sweet that was. Then he said he had someone with him (another doctor) and he wanted to show the doctor the work he had done. And would I mind letting the other doctor see the sutures. Of course, do I look presentable? (I had just woken up). He said, "Well, you have a severe case of bedhead, but he won't mind." Later, the cast was traded in for a black boot up to my knee. I was non-weight-bearing for six months! I hardly missed any work. I got driven to work, then I used crutches to get to and from the office. I worked my desk job just fine. I even went on a business trip to Chicago. Now, that made me a little nervous since it was snowing in Chicago and I didn't have studs on the bottom of my crutches. But I went to my business meetings and to and from the airport without much of a hitch. There was, however, this one time when we were all scrambling to get out of the warm office and onto the bus to make our way back to the airport. A co-worker brushed right by me for the door, which then closed on me. She didn't even hold the door open for me. I needed to push the door open but I had both of my hands on my crutches. As I started to move the door with my nose and face and head, a kind person got in front of me and held the door open so I could get out to the waiting bus. As I walked by the pushy co-worker, I thought to myself, "Seriously? Who does that?"

After getting the boot taken off and starting to walk again, I did ski again. But now it wasn't as much fun as before because I now had a titanium rod and a screw in my ankle. I had a new fear of the hills and I took it very easy. And as B. B. King might say, the thrill was gone. It was just as well. The lift tickets were getting so expensive, I knew it was time to let it go.

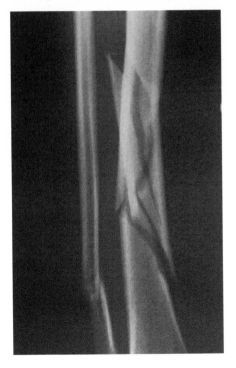

My broken leg X-rays. Bill had our Christmas cards made from this X-ray that year. It said, "On Donner, on Blitzen, on skis, on crutches. Happy Holidays, Bill and Rebecca."

As supervisors, we had to do annual recurrent emergency training (RET), which was just like the flight attendants did. This was especially nerve wracking because we were not on airplanes every day like the flight attendants were. Prior to RET, however, a dear co-worker and I took our initial training together. All was going well until we boarded a big aircraft and were told the slides would be deployed out of an aircraft door. We would have to jump out of a perfectly good airplane. Cross your arms, keep your feet straight out in front of you....and jump. When you get to the bottom, get up and move to the side. We were all lined up and ready to go at the trainer's words, "Go, go, go." One right after another. Much like zip lining, you think you can jump but we both finally had to ask someone to just push us out. I'm not afraid of heights but looking out of that door down to the end of the slide, looked like we were as high up as a three-story building. We weren't so we both got pushed out. We made it and we both passed with flying colors.

The RET recreated how you would brace for landing in a real emergency. You leave everything behind, and run out of the plane and jump down the slide. You even get into a raft in water, cut the line, and find the supplies to help you survive until assistance comes. Whoever was in charge of this training program did a very good job. It was so real with the captain speaking, lights flashing, lights going out – a real adrenalin rush. When I retired, however, I really did not mind not having the stress of always having to pass RET to continue in our jobs.

We were so anxious and excited to fly on a pass to New York City to see a play on Broadway -- any play. Our first choice was to see "Grease." Of course, we didn't buy tickets in advance because we never knew if we were going to end up in New York City or show up in Denver, Colorado. We were able to hop a flight to New York City, and once there we searched for those kiosks on the street where you can get cheap(er) tickets. Even in the 70s, seeing a play seemed pricey. So Grease was sold out. Okay, what else can we see? There were some tickets to a rock opera, Jesus Christ Superstar, and it was off Broadway. We bought two tickets to see a play that we knew nothing about, but that would change my life forever. To say that the play rocked our worlds is an understatement. We fell in love with the music, the actors, the scenes, everything. Since that time, we have seen the play at least seven times, from off Broadway plays to community theatre versions. We have never been disappointed. I've been a huge fan of Ted Neeley, who portrayed Jesus for twenty some odd years in New York. He's 74 years young. We even had a close friend at the time who played the part of King Herod in a local regional theatre. He chose to play Herod as a greasy Las Vegas slime ball! In a sequined turquoise suit, no less. We have watched the 70s movie version on television countless times, maybe a dozen. I doubt if we would ever have gone to New York City just to see a play if I wasn't working for an airline. I feel so very fortunate and grateful.

* * * * *

W<small>E TOOK A FLIGHT ON ANOTHER CARRIER WHERE WE ACTUALLY BOUGHT A TICKET.</small> We were traveling with another couple and needed to be there at the same time they arrived, for our pickup. We were flying Economy Class, and we heard a kid crying in the boarding area. Bill, whispered, "I'll probably be sitting next to that crying kid." It was a self -fulfilling prophecy. The aircraft had three- across seating. There was Bill, the kid (on a lap) and mom and dad. Since we had paid for our ticket and there wasn't a dress code to worry about, Bill was wearing beige shorts. Seriously, Bill, beige shorts on a flight? Oh my. He got up to go to the lavatory in the back of the airplane and the little kid put his chocolate cookie on Bill's temporarily empty seat. Bill came back and promptly sat down on the chocolate cookie. He had a funny look on his face and I asked him what was wrong. He stood up and his entire backside was covered in chocolate. It looked mighty suspicious and highly embarrassing. He ran back to the lavatory, took off his shorts and washed off as much of the cookie as he could. He came back with wet underwear and wet shorts and a handful of paper towels to sit on and wick off the wetness. He had, what many of our sailing friends call, "boat ass." You know, like sitting on a wet seat on a boat. While he was trying to dry off, the flight attendant came by to pick up his almost-empty beer glass. She accidentally spilled beer on the front of his shorts. Back to the lavatory to wash them again, only to return again to sit in damp clothing. It was all I could do to not laugh out loud. Our two friends were seated in the same cabin but nearer the front and I had to share the saga with them, just so they could come back to his passenger seat and give Bill a hard time. And they did! When we got to our destination, the first thing Bill did was to jump into the hotel's pool, clothes and all.

Another time I was walking onto the plane and we were backlogged walking through the First Class cabin trying to get to our Economy seats. I made eye contact with a lovely lady and we both smiled. I had a moment of recognition but quickly thought that it was one of my lovely mature flight attendants in my group. She said hello and we briefly chatted while I was at a standstill. She whispered, "Do you know who I am?" I told her she looked like a celebrity. She laughed and whispered, "I'm Pattie LaBelle." "Of course you are!" I immediately said. She told me she had a good take on people, and she said she knew that I was a good person just by looking at me. What an absolutely lovely compliment! I thanked her and moved on to the back of the plane.

I was seated next to a young man and I just couldn't help but say, "Did you know that Patti LaBelle is sitting in First Class?" He said that yes, he did know. Then he continued to tell me about a young singer, Landau Eugene Murphy, Jr., who had been a finalist in America's Got Talent the night before. Landau had asked Patti LaBelle to sing a duet with him. What a brave man he was to do that. And what a great sport Patti was to agree to join him onstage. I later saw it on TV and it was very good and afterwards she applauded him and walked off stage so he could get all of the attention. Yes, what a humble woman she is.

When we got off the airplane, I saw Patti standing there with her family. They were waiting for us! Seriously. She came up to us, introduced us to her sister and son and I introduced her to Bill. She hugged us and we went our separate ways. I will always appreciate that. She was so very kind and down to earth.

Then there was my solo trip to Narita, Japan. I was onboard doing an observation flight where I liked to say, "I'm looking to catch a flight attendant doing something right." Then I commended them for it. It was also an opportunity to see how the service was working for our customers. Sometimes we uncovered an even better way of doing the service.

When on a layover, I was usually on my own which is fine. The flight attendants do their own thing and the supervisor does his/her own thing. Besides, you might come in with a particular crew and they have an extra day layover, or you do. Then you might fly home with another crew. So that's why they are on their own and I am on my own. Now, as I've mentioned, I was at my tallest height of 5'10 ½" by this time and I was wearing high heels (in the 90s). That would make me around 6' 1" tall. I was walking down a street and I kept hearing "click" "click" "click". I turned around to see what it was and a few very small Japanese men in business suits were taking my picture. They probably had never seen such a big woman before. I smiled and let them click away. I was actually flattered.

While on my trips to Japan, I tried to do many different things each and every time. I once walked into a Buddhist Temple and sat on the floor and "listened" to a Buddhist service. Listened is probably not the right word. It was in Japanese and I couldn't understand a single word. But I sat through it (it was beautiful) and absorbed the chanting. It was very peaceful. Afterwards there was an optional silent walk through their botanical gardens. It was breathtaking and it felt so serene. And then there was the shopping. You couldn't really take too much home because of the space restrictions, but I did purchase two red and glossy black bento boxes. I still have them in my home.

Speaking of being tall, it was in the 80s when Bill and I went to Switzerland and other European countries. Switzerland was at the top of our list because we were going to meet some relatives on my father's side of the family – many we had never met before. We flew there and then took a cab ride to the train. We then took the train as far as we could until we saw a big hill. We were told that our destination was up and over the hill in a lovely valley. We transferred to a mountain rail car, which seemed to pull us up and over a steep hill. It was somewhat like a slow roller coaster. There were actual servers onboard and they came around with a cart selling salami, cheeses, and wine. It was amazing to see all the views unfold. And since it was in the 1980s, I had these adorable platform shoes in red, yellow, and pink. I was seeing eye level with Bill in these enormous shoes so I must have been 6'3" if that is possible. So I take in a breath of the lovely town of Bellinzona. As I stepped off the mountain rail car, I caught my platform heel in the grooves of the metal stairs. I did a face plant and went down like a greased refrigerator. "Welcome to Switzerland," Bill yelled and then ran over to help me. We made some hotel reservations and started to plan our call to our Zia (aunt) Lucia who did not speak English. But first we went to a café for some coffee. It was so strong that we quickly learned to ask for café Americano, a much less harsh cup of joe. A striking woman walked by us and made eye contact with me and smiled. She had a gold tooth that I noticed immediately. In fact, a lot of people were looking at us. We overheard a couple of people calling us "Grande Americanos," but in a clearly flattering way. I guess we do look like the Americans we are. We met up with our Zia Lucia at her home and somehow made conversation with pointing, expressions, and charades. She promised to have us over to meet some relatives in a few days. So we walked around the town, had dinners in wonderful places and coffee in many cafes. Maybe on two more occasions, we saw the lady with the gold tooth. "Small town," I thought. But it was so beautiful and clean in these towns. We were staying nearby in Bellingzona.

My paternal grandfather was born in Gorduno, Switzerland and my paternal grandmother was born in Camorino. My grandparents came to

America as young adults separately. Here in America, my grandmother got a job in Inverness, California as a maid, and my grandfather was hired as a ranch hand at the very same ranch. That is where they met up, never knowing one another when they were growing up in Switzerland. They had lived within maybe five minutes of one another. When we finally met up with the famiglia in Switzerland, we met person after person, and figured out who was on whose side of the family. And then we met the lady with the gold tooth! She was one of our cousins. They all kept commenting on how tall we were. That just made us stand up even taller and have much better posture. And they kept pointing to my eyelashes. I was wearing false eyelashes on a daily basis (everyone it seemed was wearing them in those days) and they seemed mesmerized by them. Or maybe one of them had fallen halfway off and it looked like I had a spider on my face! I'll never know. But what a gorgeous trip. We decided to stay one more night at our hotel, which was named House of the People in Swiss/Italian. We were up in our room with our Italian dictionary of terms trying to piece together the sentence, "We'd like to stay at the hotel one more night". When we thought we had perfected it, we marched downstairs to the hotel lobby and slowly said what we had been practicing. "Huh?" the receptionist seemed to say. We said it again. With a puzzled look, she told us to hold on and she would get someone from the back room to assist us. Out came this blonde surfer-looking dude and we spoke our sentence in English. "Oh, you want to stay another night. Totally cool." After seeing the surprised look on our faces, he said, "I'm from Manhattan Beach, California. I'll tell the receptionist."

On one lovely trip to Europe, we took a tour where we were bussed to all of the wonderful places we might not otherwise have seen. One of the most exciting trips was to Vatican City where we got to see the Pope. At the time, it was Pope John Paul II, I believe. My grandmother was still alive and she was thrilled to hear that I was "meeting" the Pope, since she was a devout Catholic and went to church EVERY day! No kidding. Well, all of us kids remember the game "telephone." Someone said something to one person, that person told someone else, who told someone else. The conversation winds up entirely different than what the first person had said. We had that happen. So our tour bus arrived at the very full Vatican Square where the Pope was speaking to everyone in Italian. The minute we got out, the Pope changed to English (we thought it was for our own personal behalf, although how would he know? -- oh wait, he's the Pope). The crowd was so large that he was the size of the head of a pin and we were far back in the crowd. Somehow the word back to the family was that we had met the Pope and by the time the much-told story got back to my grandmother, we had "kissed his ring". She was elated.

Everyday was a new adventure. We packed our bags at night and left them just outside our door (boy, were we ever trusting). The next morning the bags would be on the tour bus and we would hop onboard, awaiting our next new adventure. It sure takes the sting out of trying to figure out what to see next, and then finding your way there. And finding a vehicle to take you there. We would rotate our seats every day, so you could get a different view out of the bus windows. Well, that was fine until one of the kids caught a bad cold. He was sneezing and snotting up a storm and as each day unfolded, he would move to another seat and "slime" that window. The unsuspecting passenger would sit where he was sitting, sometime laying their tired heads on the window itself. And the next day we had two more sick people, then four, and so on. When we got to "Typhoid Larry's" original seat, we wiped it down so we wouldn't get sick too.

The last night of the very special tour, we all went to dinner in a place that basically opened up just for us. It was their day off and some arrangements had been made since there were so many of us. We had befriended a lovely Italian young lady traveling with her mom. Yes, they were Italian, but the young gal was born in Australia so she had an Aussie/Italian accent, if that's possible. We called her mother Mama Mia. The daughter was very cute and her accent was very different. The mom looked like a typical Italian mama, elderly (we thought). She was wearing a black bun hairdo, no makeup, long black clothing, sensible nun's shoes, and a shawl.

It was only after talking to them for a few days that we found out Bill and I were older than the Italian mama. But we look so young, we both thought. So there we were in the restaurant, when for some reason (probably wine was involved), I decided to do the "hang a spoon on your nose" game, which I am very good at, if I do say so myself. I can hang the spoon on my nose and walk around, even dance a little, without it falling off. The secret (should anyone care) is to exhale on the spoon much like you do when cleaning your glasses, before hanging it on your nose. Also clean the oil off your nose first. And maybe just slightly tilt your head back. That's the trick! I know many of you are trying to do that right now! Well, the next thing I knew we had Australian, Indian, French, and Italian people all trying it. It was a hoot. Then the young Italian/Australian lady was trying to hang the spoon on her nose, unsuccessfully. As beautiful as she was, she did have a rather prominent nose. The waiter ran into the kitchen and came out with a large soup spoon for her. (Oh no, he didn't). We were aghast, but she found it funny, thankfully.

Our new Aussie/Italian acquaintance with her Mama Mia

* * * * *

In our onboard services office, we would occasionally have a conference call with supervisors from Paris, Japan, London, Chicago, New York, etc. We would have to pick a time and date when the majority of the supervisors were on duty so as to make it worthwhile. Now, when you have your crazy, fun bunch of supervisors all crammed in a room listening to others, you get a little silly after awhile. It's business for the first hour, however. We were on an unusually long conference call when everyone was chiming in from all over the world, and we started in with our antics. There was one supervisor, a female, with a very low voice, from France, who always sounded like she was breathlessly inhaling a cigarette when she spoke. She probably was. We would mimic a pretend cigarette holder with a burning cigarette attached to it. We would start giggling, as quietly as we could, without getting in trouble. Another supervisor had such a drawl in her voice, that she sounded, well, drunk. I had hoped she wasn't but she sure sounded like she was. We would tilt our heads back, hold up one hand like throwing back a drink, and again start giggling. I will bet you anything that they were in Paris, or Chicago, or wherever, doing the same thing to the supervisors from New York, or San Francisco.

I was working a flight from San Francisco to Chicago, Illinois. I was going to work the Economy section on this particular trip. When we fill in for a flight attendant, we give them the time off with pay. This is sort of a thank you for doing a great job for our customers and our airline. The First Class flight attendants were all a-buzz about something. I asked them what was so exciting. They told me that B. B. King was going to be on their flight and he was putting "Louise," his precious guitar, in checked baggage. I half expected him to buy a seat for Louise but he was comfortable with checking his guitar. So when he was onboard, we took a brief moment to say hello and introduce ourselves. He was very humble, a very nice man. I proceeded to the back to work and when I went into the galley, the flight attendants were telling me that B. B. King's entire entourage was onboard in the Economy Class. They were a very fun loving, very kind group of mostly guys. They chatted us up and before the end of the flight, they gave us all tickets to see their concert that very night in town. We thanked them profusely. Alas, our layover was such that we could not make it to the show. I do regret this as that would have been my only opportunity to see them live and in person.

Sometimes when we were working at the airport and not flying, we would work the "gates." That just meant that we were nearby several flights before the boarding of our passengers. We walked on board and saw if the flight attendants needed anything. We asked them if catering had delivered exactly what they needed, or if there was an issue that needed to be resolved. This one day, I was working the gates and another supervisor told me she was needed in a meeting and couldn't get planeside to present a flight attendant with her fifteen-year service pin. (This is presented to employees with 15 years of employment and other milestone anniversaries). She asked me if I would present it for her. Of course. I'm already down there anyway. I looked on the in-flight crew list and saw that one of my new hire flight attendants was working this trip also. What a good opportunity to say hello and see how he is doing. And I can present the pin to the other flight attendant in front of her co-workers. So I walked to the gate, got down the jetway (and this is where it gets unfortunate.) I spot my new-hire barely standing up at the aircraft door. As he is sliding down the door, he yells "Hi ya, Becky!" Oh no. He's drunk. I asked him if he was feeling all right and then asked him to sit down for a moment while I talked to the Captain. I knocked on the cockpit door and spoke to the Captain. "We have an intoxicated flight attendant on board and I have to get him off the airplane before the customers start arriving." He told me to do what I needed to do. So then I talked to the Purser on the flight. She said they knew he was drunk but didn't know what to do. They had decided they would have him go to the last row in economy, they would put a blanket over him and let him sleep it off. However, he was already standing at the jetway/airplane door ready to greet our customers! I could just see him waking up mid-flight and walking around the aircraft shit-faced. I told her I had to take him off the flight and she then agreed. Usually that would mean calling up Crew Scheduling and getting a replacement flight attendant, based on the flight loads. The flight loads were such that day that the Purser insisted that the remaining flight attendants onboard could get the job done with one less flight attendant. Good call because we might have taken a delay while looking for a replacement. Getting this intoxicated new hire up to the domicile was no easy feat. He kept ducking into bathrooms where I could not go in. I'll bet he was drinking a lot of water. He probably thought he would have less alcohol in his system when he had to be alcohol tested. I'm not certain that it works that way, however. I stuck close by to him when walking so our customers could not see him swaying because he was, after all, in full uniform. I finally got him upstairs and another management person had to agree with me that he appeared drunk. Well, the sad story is that he was drunk. He was fired since he was still on probation and I never learned what happened to him after that. I do hope he got some help. I never got around to presenting that fifteen-year anniversary pin to the young lady that day.

The best and the worst thing about working in Onboard Services was that no two days were alike ever. One day you were working pre-departure at an international flight and nothing was going badly. All the flight attendants showed up, all the catering was onboard, everyone was getting along, and the flight buttoned up smoothly and had an on time departure. Another day, you were working a seemingly simple pre-departure flight to Los Angeles. Flight attendants might have been missing or late, the cockpit crew hadn't shown up from an inbound flight, customers were yelling at the customer service agents, the flight was severely oversold, and then the flight cancelled. You just never know!

We had drug testing for all employees. I thought this was a very good idea. We, as supervisors, would sometimes meet an inbound flight and ask randomly selected flight attendants to accompany us to the area where we did BAT (breath alcohol testing) and the drug testing (which we sometimes referred to as the "whiz quiz"). It was mandated but we always saw the faces of the flight attendants when the aircraft door opened and we were standing there. They knew we were ready to meet with the purser to advise them who had been selected as the winner of today's lottery. They would moan and groan as some of them commuted to and from San Francisco from different cities and had hoped to run from the airplane gate to their homebound gate/trip. It was a little disruptive to them, but they always complied. They had to. So did we. We would be in the office working away, minding our own business. Our Managers would drop in to our cubicles and ask us to go to the medical department for drug testing. I didn't mind as I knew I would be fine. I have never taken an illegal drug and hope that to always be the case. And, surprisingly, I was a teenager in the 60s when illegal drugs were the rage. I really took to heart the black and white film shown in our high school gym class, "Reefer Madness." It showed the down side of taking drugs and it shook me to the core. Beside, my parents said they'd "kill me" if I did drugs! I was nothing if not obedient.

* * * * *

We LIVED IN EL GRANADA, CA FOR OVER 20 YEARS. We regularly commuted to work (me, to the airport, Bill to the city). We would head north to Pacifica, over to Daly City, and on to the airport. It was a decent commute, sometimes with traffic, sometimes not. However, the Devil's Slide area (between Montara and Pacifica) had mud slides fairly often which washed away the roads. The roads were impassable and they had to be closed. When that happened, we had to drive south to Half Moon Bay, turn left, go over Route 92 to San Mateo, and north to the airport. That route more than doubled our commute and the roads had twice the number of people as usual. This particular year, the slide was washed away for several months (a tunnel has since been built), but sadly not before our beloved Montara Chart House went out of business as a result of the closed road.

I suggested we use the commute time to learn Spanish from language tapes. I'm half Latina, so I needed to, I figured. There were some airline language tapes in our domicile, available for borrowing. I got us a couple of cassette tapes. Anyone remember those? The airline language tapes included mostly what to say on a flight, how to greet customers, what the words were for things like "ticket", "baggage", etc. It was fun and my Caucasian husband enjoyed learning Spanish. He so wanted to try out some phrases on my Mexican mom (who spoke Spanish and English fluently). The day came and my mom came by to visit us. Bill greeted her in his best Spanish and offered her a beverage. She was thrilled. He then said a few more phrases that he had learned. She smiled at him while sipping her drink, and finally said, "That was so nice to be greeted in Spanish but why did you ask me to put my seat in an upright position for take off?" We laughed a lot over that one.

* * * * *

STANDING BY FOR A FLIGHT IS FUN, ADVENTUROUS, AND SOMETIMES HECTIC, BUT NEVER BORING. I refuse to do boring. We were standing by at the gate for a flight to somewhere and they kept paging two First Class customers by name, to no avail. It was nearing departure time and Bill and I knew we were at the top of the standby list. Was it wrong to hope that paying customers do not make their scheduled flight so we can get their seats? Maybe, but we were so hoping to get into First Class and just to be on the flight. Then they called our names! "Party of two, Newlin!" There we were onboard being ushered to our seats, row 1A and 1B! Oh, the joy of savoring First Class. The flight attendant magically appeared and offered some pre-departure champagne. Heck yes, we thought. We started to sip our champagne when the ominous gate agent came onboard and started walking up to us. "Uh oh." I said to Bill, "Drink up, I think they are taking us off." So we downed the champagne and the gate agent whispered that the paying customers had finally shown up right at departure. Technically, at departure time, paying customers do not have to be accommodated because it is so close to departure time (within five minutes). But this day, this gate agent probably thought that since the plane was still at the gate, and the aircraft door was still open, that they would try to accommodate them. It beats getting yelled at by the customer after the jetway is pulled and the plane leaves. So we grabbed our meager belongings (remember, we take very little) and came off of the airplane. Those were, after all, their reserved seats and they had paid for them. At least we got a glass of champagne out of it. So, we returned to a now vacant boarding area and sat back down. We watched as the doors closed and the plane left.

Earlier I mentioned that we almost got to fly First Class and almost got seats 1A and 1B. Well, the airline folks call one of the First Class seats, the "Shakespeare" seat. That is row 2B, as in "2B or not 2B, that is the question". I did not make this up.

On another such flight in First Class where we actually got to stay onboard, we were offered a pre-departure beverage. I said I'd like some champagne. The flight attendant judgingly looked at her watch and said "Okay". It was 9:00 a.m. Hey, we were on vacation and it was 5:00 p.m. somewhere!

When we used to call ahead to be put on a standby list, the person on the other end of the phone would tell us the loads. They would say there are zero seats in economy, three seats in business class, and/or two seats in First Class, as an example. Sometimes they would tell us, "There's no way you'll get on this flight, it is severely oversold." Sometimes we took their word for it, but other times, we just showed up to take our chances. You just never knew. Sometimes there are plenty of seats for all of the standby's in the gate area and all of a sudden, up to the gate comes a group from another cancelled flight, and you are just out of luck.

There are other times when the flight is oversold and there appears to be no chance in hell of being offered a seat. Then the connecting flight coming in with passengers for this flight is delayed and passengers are transferred to a later flight. This is done so that this flight can go out on time. Then all of those passengers don't show up and standby's get on, sometimes even in First Class.

When we don't get on a flight, we can play games, read books, read magazines, play on our computers and cell phones. Oh yeah, and talk to one another. When we ran out of things to do, we would see that a flight was due to arrive in, say, five minutes at a particular gate. One of us would sneak up to the area near the arriving gate door. One of us would stay seated. When the arriving gate door opened and people started spilling out, one of us would blend into the arriving crowd. Upon seeing our loved ones, we would run up to each other and hug and kiss like everyone else was doing. That was in the old days when ordinary people could come to the airport and wait for their friends and family right at the arriving gate. That always took up five to ten minutes. Then we would go back to our books/magazines, computers, or just plain ol- fashioned talking. Once in a while, there would be one of those stores in the airport that had those loungers with the vibrating seats and leg massagers. We could burn up a half hour sitting in them. Like I say, it was never boring and there was always something to do. You just have to look for it, like browsing in magazine/newspaper stores for half an hour or more.

Then there was the time that we didn't have plans for Christmas in California. We were talking to another couple (who don't work for the airlines) and they said they felt like taking off on Christmas Day and just going somewhere. We decided right there on the spot to go to New York City for Christmas time. We decided to travel on Christmas Day itself. Now that really is a good time to travel for an employee, an eligible, and a companion or two. Everyone who needs to be somewhere for Christmas, is already there. So the 767 was nearly empty. We stood by for the flight and also provided two companion passes for the other couple. Bill and I were boarded in First Class and our companions were boarded in Business Class (which is just as nice as First Class in my opinion). Both classes of service offered you complimentary champagne and a nice meal. It was a lovely flight. Not knowing where to stay, we just checked out the layover hotel for the flight crew and flight attendants. It was the Leona Helmsley hotel right in downtown. As we were looking for a way to get to the hotel, a flight attendant yelled to us with Christmas glee, "Come with us in the layover van." Wow, what timing, what luck. We four crammed into the van with the pilots and flight attendants. Everyone was in such a good mood on the ride over to the hotel. We got our rooms and then hit the town running. While there, we got four New York Yankee hats and immediately started talking with a pretty bad New York accent and a newfound New York attitude. We saw the skaters in Central Park. We saw the Rockettes perform. They were last minute tickets that we secured and we all had different seats, but nowhere near one another. That was really okay as we were so mesmerized with the holiday show that we wouldn't have talked to one another anyway.

It was very cold there but we all had mittens and gloves – and hats. Except Dana. He had little cold weather gear and wouldn't get any, stubborn boy. Then we saw people in ear warmers, and we said "buy one of those." No way, he said. But a few minutes later, we observed him at a kiosk purchasing a set of ear warmers from a street vendor. Now he was a happy boy. We piled a lot of last minute things into those couple of days we were there. I still marvel at how easy it was to travel to New York City on a pass on Christmas Day. Shhhhhh, don't tell anyone!

A motley crew in New York one Christmas

It was a very different story trying to get from San Francisco to Los Angeles a few days before Thanksgiving. Very different. There were San Francisco-Los Angeles flights almost hourly. There were hundreds of "standby" employees and eligibles. The agents were able to board one or two – or none, on each departing flight. The gaggle of standby's wasn't really dwindling. Then, and this was really a holiday miracle, because it seldom happens. The gate agents announced that there would be a special added flight to LAX which they called the Super Shuttle to Los Angeles. They filled a 747 with ALL of the employees/eligibles and maybe a paying passenger or two. Oh what a festive flight it was. With one hour to serve a beverage to hundreds of people, it was actually accomplished. Flight attendants filled an entire tray of sodas and handed the tray to the first row. We just passed the tray ourselves to the person on our right and took a beverage if we wanted one. Not many choices to choose from (cola and 7-up) but no one seemed to care. We were on our way to Los Angeles. Ah, the good old days.

A newly retired flight attendant shared her story on Facebook about how much she enjoyed working as a flight attendant. I asked her if I could use it. She said yes.

"On December 6, 1967 this small town girl from Yuma, Arizona, embarked on "the career of a lifetime". Today, I would have completed fifty years of flying. I had my twenty-second birthday the second day of stew school, my first Christmas and New Year's away from home and family! Wow! What a life it was! I loved every minute of it…even the bad days I usually found a way to laugh about it and yes there were a few days I even shed a couple of tears. I met so many wonderful people, and went to so many places, some exotic and some not (like one Thanksgiving in Des Moines, Iowa). It was all such a fantastic experience. During this time I married Tom (forty-seven years ago now), had two incredible sons, now I have two really super daughters-in-law, and now six beautiful grandchildren. During this time I had four businesses, sometimes getting in from an International Trip only to hit the bricks to run my businesses without even taking a nap. Along the way, I met some of the most fascinating friends who were flight attendants and pilots, many of whom I'm still in touch with. We'd share jumpseats, more meal services than I could possibly count, great stories, laughed at each other's stories and cried and laughed together through it all. Through it all, I never failed to be grateful for the opportunities it offered me, which is why I miss you all more than you could ever know. Think of me once in awhile and have a Tsing Tao beer for me while shopping at Science & Tech in Shanghai, but most of all, think of me when you are hauling so much stuff home that when you get home with it, you wonder what made you buy all that stuff! Safe flying and God Bless."

That really sums it up from a flight attendant's perspective. Mine is a little different perspective as it would still be from other employee's recollections. All different, and that's wonderful.

It was one particular Christmas time at the airport, where I was working as a gate supervisor. This is the time when some flight attendants might push the limits of our regulation uniform rules. Most flight attendants were beautifully coiffed and properly attired. However, sometimes you came across one flight attendant who was in the Christmas spirit big time. One of our job descriptions was to address any and all violations of the uniform dress code. So I am happily walking through the festive San Francisco Airport, when what to my eyes did I see? It was a flight attendant in uniform all right. But she was also wearing reindeer antlers on her head, blinking lights as a necklace, and lots of red and green. I first thought maybe she was a "plant" to see if we were doing our jobs in addressing non-regulation flight attendants. I couldn't NOT walk by without saying something. So I said hello, identified who I was and asked her if I could chat with her for a moment. I went through my diplomatic mantra of saying we know the holiday is festive, however, we still have to represent our airline in the most favorable light. I suggested that she should not be walking through the airlines all lit up like that. She listened to me, and then smiled. "I don't work for your airline." What? I looked closely and saw that she was indeed in another airline's uniform. I was so embarrassed and she seemed to revel in the fact that I had made such a glaring error. So, all I could say was, "You are right! Have a wonderful day, and Merry Christmas." I walked into our office with my face still red and burning hot.

As long as flight attendants were in regulation uniform for takeoff and landing, if it was a holiday, and they donned Santa hats, well, that really is kind of cute, and festive. So our airline didn't have too much of a problem with that. But we would ask our flight attendants to be in perfect regulation uniform while walking to and from the aircraft. Other customers see us and if they like what they see (perfectly groomed flight attendants) they may even book a flight with us in the future. And the uniform regulations for take-off and landing are obviously for safety reasons as well. Of course, we don't want them to be clones. We like their individuality. As we all know, we all come in different shapes, sizes, and colors. I think that's wonderful.

A breathtaking thing I saw recently, however, was a large group of Asian, lovely, female flight attendants en route to their respective flights. There may have been twenty-five ladies walking by in a hotel lobby in Los Angeles. I was just struck by how they appeared to all be the same age, same height, and same weight. They all had the same black, very neat pony-tails to go with their beautiful uniforms. Everyone was staring, they looked that good. That just struck me as a lovely look. But I also appreciate that our airline is a diverse carrier, as well.

The joy of pass travel (standby) is fun because you get to go to many places you didn't even know of. We have an old close friend (who was an usher in our wedding almost forty-eight years ago). He was (and still is) a wanderer, always working and living all over the world. He had a boat and he and his family sailed around the world. At 71, he still needs to always be on the go, when some of us are content to have a routine of some sorts in our lives. In the old days of no texting, e-mailing, or cell phones, we notified one another mostly by U. S. mail. We got a letter from him saying that in April of that particular year, his boat was going to arrive in Antigua,

West Indies. He and his girlfriend were going to be there for five days. He wanted us to fly there and join them on their vacation.

Wow, that will be fun, we thought. Well, it was a wonderful adventure. We would never have thought to go there for no other reason than it just hadn't crossed our mind. We arrived a day ahead of their planned arrival and got our hotel. We went to the pool, walked around, and had a wonderful dinner. We loved this new-found place. It was so different than any spot we had been to up to that point. So the next day, we spent another lovely day in paradise. At around three p.m., we walked to the boat dock and sat there watching for his boat to come in. We sat there chatting, dangling our feet in the water, until nightfall. We then decided they were probably now arriving the next day. We went to dinner and generally painted the town red. They had casinos and everything that a big cosmopolitan city would have, but still with a beachy feel. We aren't gamblers, but I love to people-watch (airports or casinos), so we did just that. The third day, we swam in our pool, and then we rented a little cute sailboat. We just sailed around the bay and thoroughly enjoyed that. Again, around three p.m., we went back to the boat dock. No sign of them. Oh well, we're still having fun. And if it weren't for his invite, we never would have been there. Day five we packed up and came home, saying to one another that we were sorry to have missed them. But what a wonderful vacation we just had. A few weeks after we arrived home, we got a snail-mail letter from our friend, back dated to a week or so before we would have left California. He wrote that his plans had changed and he would NOT be in Antigua, after all. The U.S. mail is pretty decent, but when you write a letter on a boat, you have to wait for some time to get somewhere on land where you can post a letter. That was the reason for the time lag. We didn't mind at all.

Now this is the same dear friend who built waterfalls for many beautiful hotels and resorts all over the world. When he wasn't building, he was sailing, diving, or surfing. One time we just happened to know that he was in Acapulco, Mexico building waterfalls for the Acapulco Princess Hotel. Now, the Princess was an elaborate hotel/resort that looked so beautiful on paper. We called his mother and said that we wanted to go visit him and stay a few days, but we wanted to surprise him. So she gave us all the details of where he would be, and his room number. We stood by for a flight to Mexico City and got right on. Woo hoo! Once in Mexico City we found our way to Acapulco and took a cab to the Acapulco Princess. In those days, many hotels gave discounts to airline employees (I hope they still do as it was such a perk -- and if the room is going to be empty anyway, why not?) This particular hotel gave us a (wait for it!) 90% off discount. We ended up paying only 10% of the cost of the hotel. As we drove up we noticed teal-colored peacocks on the grounds of the hotel with their feathers fully fanned out and beautifully bright. It was a stunning white hotel, where the lobby was both indoors and outdoors. The valet and hotel staff all had startlingly white, crisp uniforms. They were breathtaking, actually. We were shown our room (right across from Jack and his girlfriend's room). We did not see them that night. Our plan was to hang out at breakfast, which was served on a gorgeous outdoor patio under clear blue skies. Again, stunning. When we spotted them walking to breakfast, right out of a cheesy B movie, we put up our newspapers to shield us from them. They sat down very close to our table. When they were all settled in, we pulled down our newspaper and said, "Hello, Jack." He was so surprised and glad to see us. Good thing as we had come a long way to see them. Now, I mentioned that we said "Hello, Jack," because as we airline employees know, one can never say "Hi Jack," especially in an airport. Yes, even back in the 70s, that word was forbidden. People would be taken off an airplane before departure if that word was heard.

We stayed in Acapulco for a week. With our friend being the supervisor, for that week, he assigned jobs to his workers. Then he was pretty free for the day, just occasionally checking in with his crew. He was getting paid for his job, and also for their room and two free meals a day. Our generous friend used one meal for the two of them. He then offered us the other free meal for the two of us. We have never forgotten his generosity. The boys surfed in the morning, while gals read or went to the pool. Then we had the whole day, everyday, to ourselves, sometimes going out nearby on a small boat. It was a fabulous vacation and we did it quite reasonably, which was important to us in those days.

This same friend went on to become an International Boat Captain, and inherited a quarter of a lovely hotel in Mazatlan, when his grandfather passed away. And yes, he invited us to use his Penthouse for a week (complimentary-holy cow), and that was fairly recently. That was a story right out of the movies. It was a crazy, fun vacation that I must tell you about.

We, and another couple, were offered the Penthouse at our friend's hotel in Mazatlan. He was living in a condo nearby where his good buddy also lived. We checked into our Penthouse, which was really huge. Our friends took half and we took the other half. We couldn't even see them unless we met in the big living room, or on the huge patio overlooking the ocean. Oh my.

Our host's only daughter was pregnant and wanted to be in Mexico for the birth. On the very day that we arrived, our friend was becoming a grandparent for the very first time! His wife had just arrived in town for the birth, and there was excitement everywhere. People literally were running in and out of his condo and our Penthouse. We got word that the Japanese contingent of family members were arriving from Japan to meet their newest family member. (The father of the baby is Japanese.) The daughter's family wanted them to have a nice place to stay, so our host asked us to move out and go to the hotel room next door. They said our other friends could stay put and just lock off their half of the Penthouse (each half of the Penthouse had its own entrance and exit). So they stayed there and the family members from Japan moved in to the adjoining area. We were right next door in another room, which was nice and our patios were side by side. So all of this was going on while we were there. It was all good news, but really chaotic. We were exhausted by the end of the trip.

And then there was the hurricane. We had finished dinner in the indoor/outdoor restaurant and then we danced on the indoor/outdoor dance floor, with live music and some karaoke. Yes, I sang karaoke. I'm such a ham. We danced until we called it a night. We noticed as we were leaving that the wind started howling and we were very glad to get safely to our rooms. Then we got a call from the front desk. "Did you leave your purse near the dance floor?" We didn't think we did but Bill thought he would go downstairs to see, just in case it was someone's we knew. Well, by this time the hurricane was in full force, with wind blowing through the indoor/outdoor dance floor, paintings were falling off the walls, rain was coming down and going sideways. All along, the band was still playing and people were still dancing. Amazing.

We took another trip to Mazatlan with our boat Captain and his best friend. There were just the four of us. He and his cousins had built a huge home on the beach, but otherwise in the middle of nowhere. You drove on an unpaved road to their home and there was nothing in sight but a gorgeous view from their balcony. The waves were lapping at the foundation of the home. The roads were woodsy with tall plants hiding anyone from plain sight. We four were able to occupy one floor of the house. Each floor had its own entrance and exit, a balcony, three bedrooms, three bathrooms, kitchen, and living room. It was huge. Apparently the cousin owned the other floor. And still another relative occupied the third floor when he was there, which we understood wasn't often.

His cousins living there had three wild dogs which we referred to as the Hounds of Baskerville. They were untrained, aggressive, barky, and scary. They had just let them run wild their entire lives, and it showed. They were all over us when we got out of the car and since I'm allergic to most dogs, I was very wary of them and kept my distance.

Now, the boys wanted to go out surfing every morning for a few hours. I asked if it was safe for me to take walks on the beach or on the street while they were surfing. "No," I was told. The beach was so isolated that there was nowhere to run if someone approached you. And the back roads were unsafe because anything or anyone could be in the bushes and jump right out at you. Well, I didn't want that. It was either go with them at oh-dark-thirty and watch them surf for hours or stay back at the house. I could drink coffee, lounge in bed, read, shower and take my time getting dressed. Then I would be ready when they returned to go out to breakfast or lunch. And then spend the rest of the day with them. Guess what I chose? Sleeping in, reading, lounging, of course. What would you do? Our Captain friend did mention prior to leaving, "Lock all the doors, my cousin sometimes likes to come in and look around and see what's going on." He also added, "and we have also had some recent break-in's." Well, this was not going well. But I locked myself in every morning and tried to enjoy myself until they got back from surfing. I was inside the house but I heard the doors rattling as if someone was trying to get in, but couldn't. I'm thinking it was the cousin but I didn't want to find out. Thank goodness nothing occurred. But the rattling of the doors was disconcerting. I would hide in my room. But that is how it was during that time and in that particular section of town. And, darn it, I was on vacation!

We always had a good time once the boys were back from surfing. We would go into town and play tourist and just enjoy the days. Then we would come home and cook something wonderful for dinner together. There was no television (it got taken in a recent break-in). So we played board games and just had a real good time. When 5:00 p.m. rolled around, Mark would excitedly exclaim, "Time for Sun-Downers." What's that, we wondered. We had a table filled with all kind of fruit punches – orange juice, pineapple juice, guava, lemonade, you name it. And there was an assortment of adult beverages – rum, vodka, tequila, and bourbon. We would make up our own concoctions and they tasted different every night. But they were called "Sun-Downers." We would sit on the patio and sip them while the sun went down along the horizon. I wasn't frightened when I was with my hubby and the other two men we were vacationing with. By the way, I didn't really want to go back to this huge house again. Yes, it was 8,000 square feet with an ocean view and had a garage to house at least 14 cars, but it was still a scary place. And it's just as well that we didn't go back as our Captain friend decided to move out to a lovely condominium nearer to town and close to the hotel that he had a quarter interest in.

We had a rare opportunity to travel to Costa Rica via Nicaragua one July. There was an international surfing contest and Bill wanted to attend the event and participate in it. There were going to be some big name surfers attending from all over the world. We got a reservation for an all-inclusive hotel/resort in Boca Barranca. This is one of those times when it is a good thing to make advance reservations because we could get a good deal if we booked it through the surf contest people. And if we did it early. Now we just needed to get there on time, on our own airline and a partner airline (a reciprocating airline who would give airline employees of one airline a discount on another). Bill wanted/needed to bring his own surfboard. I understand that you can check golf clubs in odd-size baggage for free, but a surfboard can cost up to 200 dollars to check it – or more. So, of course, we have to abide by the rules. But still, it's 200 dollars. So we get to the San Francisco airport with surfboard in hand (or arm) in its own surfboard bag. We are waiting in line for the next available customer service agent. Joy! It's a customer service agent that I knew. We had worked together in the inflight office when she was on a special assignment at one time. She said, "Don't worry, I'll book your surfboard through to Costa Rica and back." So I had my credit card in hand to pay the 200 dollars and she said, "You're fine, put your card away." I thanked her profusely and we were on our merry way with 200 dollars still in our checkbook. What a great start to a great trip. It was a lovely adventure and we never had to worry about whether Bill's surfboard was boarded. It made it there and back, effortlessly. The surf was big and Bill said it was lots of fun. He was finished in his particular heats within a couple of days. I enjoyed the beach and watching the surfers. Oh, and hanging out with a group of handsome Brazilian boys who were also surfing. I smiled at them because they were running down the beach with their Brazilian flag. Then they were my best friends for the day. After the competition was done, we had the rest of the week to play. Bill would surf around sunset each evening and I would go out to the water's edge with a book or a magazine and a beverage and watch him surf. Nice.

Someone staying there recommended a zip line adventure. We had never done zip lining but we were willing to try. It was a blast. Now, I was the first to try it. The guide said lift your first foot off the landing and then lift the other foot. It was easy lifting my first foot off the landing, but the second foot would not lift up. "Someone push me," I said. Someone did and I was on my way. Wheeeeeeee! It was such fun. We went from short, low zip lines, and graduated to a higher level and an even higher level. It was very high up and a very long ride.

Also while there we had a rental van and took a ride into town. We were pulled over by the federales, although we didn't think we had done anything wrong. And we hadn't. They asked to see our passports which we readily had. They took their time looking them over, pausing as if waiting for us to say something. Not knowing what to say or do, we said nothing. Again, another pause. When the situation just got awkward with all the silence, they waved us on and let us go. We didn't get a ticket or anything. We got back to the resort and mentioned it to some people. It was just so odd an encounter. "You were supposed to give them money," we were told. What for? We learned that they sometimes pull over tourists and talk to them and are basically hoping for a payoff of some sort. We're so glad that ignorance is bliss because we had no idea. And we still had our wallets intact.

On one particular flight, we were standing by for a flight and there were also two very young SA's. Their parents had dropped them off and were staying with them in the boarding area until they were assured they were safely on the plane. I figured out that the parents were airline employees and eligibles and that their children were traveling as UM's (unaccompanied minors). We had no idea of the seniority of the parents. These children were decked out in their Sunday best. The little girl had a party dress on with anklet socks and black, shiny Mary Jane shoes. The little boy had slacks and a teeny jacket with a cute little bow tie. They were both precious looking and easily charmed the customer service agents. Luckily there were four available First Class seats. None of them were together but the flight attendants assured the parents that they would look after them and make sure their precious cargo was delivered to the proper people picking them up. So I was seated next to an adult. Bill was seated with the little boy, and the young girl was seated next to another lady. The service began and my seat mate and I had been given our choice of adult beverage. This was followed by a ramekin of warm (yes, warm!) nut mix – cashews, peanuts, macadamia nuts, and pecans. I got up to go say hello to Bill and his young seat mate. Well they were already chums. Bill had his beverage, the young man had his soda, and they were both coloring! They had been given crayons and some paper from a coloring book and they were both coloring up a storm -- of course knowing Bill, I know he always colors out of the lines. Me, I always had to stay within the lines! I just had to! They were really having a good time and Bill helped the young man fill the time until we landed.

*　*　*　*　*

NAPKIN FOLDING WAS AN ART ON THE AIRPLANE, ESPECIALLY IN THE PREMIUM CABINS. It was actually taught to all flight attendants. You had to have a certain type of napkin in order to make it work. If it's part polyester, it'll droop and not hold a fold. But the napkins our airline used were made out of stiff white cotton, probably starched. Flight attendants would artfully stuff them into champagne flutes. They would make fans or roses for the console as a decorative touch. Some of the more artistic flight attendants would fashion a puppet for some little kid on the flight. You know like some fancy hotels and cruise lines make elephants and teddy bears out of the towels. I could only fan fold a napkin, back and forth, and then just bend it in half. Then I would place the napkin in a wine glass and then fluff it out. That was pretty enough and the simplest trick I knew how to achieve. Not sure if this was done on the particular flight that the cute little boy and girl were on, but I'll bet it was.

*   *   *   *   *

JUST A FEW DAYS AFTER THE HORRIBLE 9/11 INCIDENT, MY NEIGH-BOR AND FRIEND ASKED ME TO ACCOMPANY HER TO WILLIAMS-BURG, VIRGINIA. She wanted to see the botanical gardens and some of the historic homes. I was a little reluctant to fly yet but figured that we all had to "get back on the horse" -- the sooner, the better. Airports were open again and yes, there was some space available for me to pass ride. My friend bought a ticket and we were lucky enough to get on the same flight. It was a nice, although subdued flight understandably. The flight attendants were friendly, senior, and quietly efficient. One senior flight attendant saw my name on the manifest (the manifest is the list of passengers who are on the flight given to them by the Customer Service agent). She noticed that I was a supervisor. She came by and quietly knelt down by my side to say hello. Then she asked if I could come back into the galley with her so we could talk. "Of course," I said and left my seat partner for a few minutes. She started to weep and said how scared she was to fly nowadays. I consoled her and we talked through it. She didn't know how she could continue flying as her chosen career. I asked her if she was at least the minimum age to retire (age fifty for flight attendants) and she said yes. I suggested to her, among other things, that early retirement might be an option. She was startled as though it had not ever entered her mind. I assured her that life was indeed great on the outside. She said she didn't have any qualifications for anything else, as she had never done anything else but be a flight atten-dant her entire adult life. I assured her she was very qualified. I mentioned that flight attendants know all about the safety of our passengers. She could work in a safety or security job. During flights, flight attendants solve issues that our customers have and calm down passengers who are nervous. She could be in a customer-oriented job. Seriously, with her handling of people and their fears, she could work for a psychologist in an office. Flight attendants also talk to customers to suggest they become frequent fliers. Then they tell them what benefits they would get with the points they acquired from being a member. She could get a job in Sales. "So," I continued, "it sounds like you are over-qualified for a number of jobs." She smiled and said she would think about it and thanked me for my time. I later got an e-mail from her that she had just put in her paperwork for retirement. I hope she is enjoying retirement and maybe volunteering or working a nice part time job.

* * * * *

A FEW TIMES A YEAR, WE, AS SUPERVISORS, WOULD ACCOMPANY THE FLIGHT ATTENDANT CREW ON A FLIGHT -- A "PERFORMANCE EVALUATION" WE CALLED IT. We openly went to their briefing and introduced ourselves, told them what our purpose was to be onboard with them (to see that the flight attendants duties were performed according to regulation and to compliment the flight attendants who went above and beyond for our customers.) If we saw mistakes, we would ask that they be corrected. We would also help out if they had an unruly passenger that they could not (or didn't want to) deal with. They might be too busy to take the time to deal with a simple, or not so simple, issue. If we could help them with these issues, they seemed to appreciate us more. Then they would understand why we were onboard. Did the pilots like us on their flights? Yes, most of them did. I would introduce myself to the cockpit crew immediately and tell them why I would be onboard today. Most were happy to see me and very, very few would admonish me to "not hassle the flight attendant crew – they know what they're doing." To that end I would assure them that I just wanted to make sure the service flow in one, two, or three cabins, was done efficiently and graciously. It usually was. And if they had a suggestion on how to make a service flow even better, I would watch and offer comments. Then I would bring the comments back to our managers for evaluation and possible change.

So on one particular flight to Europe, the Purser (the flight attendant in charge on this particular flight on this particular day) came up to me and said "The Captain wants to see you up in the cockpit." Those were the days when flight attendants and cockpit crews could walk back and forth, in and out of the cockpit. Gulp! I immediately thought "What did I do wrong?" I sheepishly knocked on the cockpit door and braced myself to face the pilot and the first officer. "Welcome," said the captain, "come and sit with us and look out at the spectacular view over Greenland. We were getting bored up here and wanted some company." I was so relieved. The view from so high up overlooking Greenland from the cockpit was like nothing I had ever seen. It was breathtaking. While I was sitting on a jumpseat in the cockpit, a flight attendant knocked on the door. She came in with three hot fudge sundaes for the Captain, First Officer, and me! Wow. That was very memorable. I was very grateful to all of them. And I wasn't in trouble, after all. That must be my Catholic guilt thinking process.

There was a time when flight attendants had to be a certain height and weight to continue to fly. I understood the height restriction – you have to be tall enough to at least reach the overhead bin. But I always felt the weight restriction was a little unfair. Yes, I realize you need to be able to fit through the emergency escape door in an emergency, but a few pounds over an ideal weight should not have mattered. A man, as an example, might be the correct height and be as slim as a reed, but works out in a gym and has gained muscle weight. He might be over the weight deemed the "maximum". Also we had older flight attendants who were just slightly plump and looked absolutely wonderful. If they were one pound over the weight maximum, we had to take them off the flights until they lost "X" number of pounds. They would come to us and stand in line while we weighed them. I thought that was a humiliating practice but it was part of my job. I know I am tall and not a skinny minny, so I certainly understood. If they were over a certain weight, we considered them (and this is not my jargon as I think it is unkind) TFTF – too fat to fly. I never used that term regarding any of my flight attendants (I think flight attendants actually made it up). However, I would work with them to take them off trips and then bring them back to flying as soon as possible. We would suggest they talk to their own doctors, etc. Sometimes a medical issue made them a little over the maximum weight. They could go over to our company Medical Department and discuss it with the doctors and then they might give them a small, temporary "weight exception" to get them back to flying. Supervisors had to weigh in as well. When it came time for me to weigh in, I panicked. Now, I'll take off my watch, shoes, earrings, anything I can, to make me weigh less. On this particular day, I had a broken leg, a titanium rod and screws in my leg, and a big, bulky shoe boot up to my knee. I weighed in TFTF. I couldn't believe it. So I went to our company medical department and told them about my "heavy" shoe boot and they gave me a temporary medical exception. My boss wasn't too pleased that I had done that, but I figured if it was good enough for flight attendants that I could do it too.

Then there was one of my fight attendants who was really a funny gal. Let's just say her name was Sha-Nay-Nay so you get a mental picture. She came upstairs to my cubicle one day just prior to weighing in and said she was dieting like crazy to be able to weigh in under the weight maximum. I asked her how she was feeling. "Hungry," she answered. "And your office desk looks just like a pork chop!" Poor dear.

I went on business trips with that broken leg, even in the snow, as I wore the crazy boot for a full six months. I walked from the parking lot to the airport, through security, and past the moving sidewalk. I was too cautious to use the moving sidewalk and didn't want to fall down at the end of it. That could back up people trying to rush to catch their flights. So I just walked the length of the huge airport and back every day. I was the most fit I had ever been in my life, but I was still too heavy to fly as a flight attendant. I couldn't take a flight attendant's place anyway with crutches and a shoe boot so it really didn't matter.

But back to the weight requirements and restrictions. There eventually was a ruling that it was a discriminatory practice and all airlines dropped that sad weight program. I just happened to see a talk show on television shortly before the weight restrictions were done away with. There was the talk show host and a panel of flight attendants from many airlines, all of them disguised in some way or another. They were wearing wigs, different colors of hair, glasses, etc. I didn't understand at the time why they couldn't just be themselves to talk about it. But there may have been some policy with some airlines that prohibited the discussion in public.

Flight attendants had an age fifty minimum requirement for early retirement. There was no maximum. As long as you could pass the recurrent emergency training and wanted to continue to fly, you could stay on. We had some very senior flight attendants. Being a flight attendant, I believe, kept them young. They were up and out with the public all dressed up and doing some hard work. One very senior flight attendant was a commuter. That means she lived in another state and would fly in the day before a trip, to be in place in San Francisco for her flight the next day. Just prior to her retirement, it was said that she flew in to San Francisco, took a nap, and when she woke up, she thought she had already taken her working trip. She just stood by for a fight back home. And she missed her scheduled trip in San Francisco entirely.

We got the reputation of having lots of senior flight attendants. One television commercial stated, "When you fly on our airline, we take you to see your grandmother." "When you fly on "their" airline, they ARE your grandmother."

We did do fun things with and for our flight attendants at times. We staged one of those "New Year, New You" kind of events for them in an area that surrounded our offices. We invited hair stylists, barbers, chair massage people, foot reflexology people, and plastic surgeons. Okay, maybe the plastic surgeons were a bit much because we received a little flack for that. Apparently some of the older flight attendants were offended that we thought they needed to have some work done! But we insisted that it was more about facials, Botox, and skin tightening creams. It sure was fun. They trimmed and styled flight attendants' hair before their flights. They gave chair massages and foot reflexology for flight attendants coming in from working and walking around on a long flight. All the business owners had their brochures from their companies to pass out to them, should they wish to come back to see them. I was pleasantly surprised to see how many flight attendants came through, from in and out of our domicile. Sometimes flight attendants have three- or four-hour-long airport layovers and this certainly gave them something wonderful to do for themselves. There was a good vibe running throughout our domicile that day and that made us feel good about having set this all up for them.

One of my flight attendants was a very tall, beautiful American of Korean descent. She was also one of my favorite people. She was a good flight attendant and she was always so nice to me. When she pronounced my name she always put the syllable in a different place. My name is Rebecca and she always called me "Reb-e-'Kah, with the emphasis on the last syllable. My co-workers loved it so much that some of them adopted my new name pronunciation.

An unfortunate car accident occurred, and she passed away from the accident. She left a small child behind. I was devastated for her family and her co-workers. Of course I needed and wanted to attend her funeral services. I went to a church in San Francisco and her entire family was there. Her mother was tearfully greeting all the attendees and saying a comforting word or two back and forth. When I got to her mother, I mentioned that I was her daughter's supervisor and she grabbed me, hugged me, and started to cry. I hugged her back and tried to comfort her. People generally have family, friends, and co-workers at their funerals, but having her daughter's boss there seemed very important. I'm so glad I went. Then it dawned on me that when my own mom passed away early in her seventies, my fellow supervisors, my own boss, and my boss's boss were all in attendance. Yes, for my mom, but mostly for my comfort. The co-workers who attended the service meant a lot to me. They took time away from the office to attend my mom's memorial. I never forgot that. So yes, I better understood how my flight attendant's mother felt.

And speaking of funerals, which is just another part of life, I attended the funeral of a very senior international flight attendant. At some point in the 80s, we acquired many flight attendants from another wonderful airline. Prior to that our flights were mostly coming and going within the United States. We also acquired some of their international routes during the merge. This flight attendant was very well thought-of and many flight attendants attended. I was sitting with them in the church, when a lady asked me about the ladies seated near me. These flight attendants (not kids anymore) looked beautifully coiffed and so very well dressed. She thought they were all super models. "They're flight attendants," I told the lady. She replied, "I knew it! They are the best dressed and most lovely people in the entire room."

*   *   *   *   *

ONE TIME, WE WANTED TO USE TWO SPACE AVAILABLE PASSES AND TAKE OUR TWO FRIENDS ON COMPANION PASSES. It really was a win-win, as the tickets for four cost us nothing and they invited us to their time-share in Kona. So the lodging cost us nothing, although we insisted we at least pay for the food. It worked out really well. We all got Economy Class and all in the same row. Now this is huge because you usually don't get on the first flight to Hawaii that you try for. You usually don't get seats all together either. Since you almost never get four seats in First Class we were very happy with our Economy seats. I knew most of the San Francisco-based crew members on this particular day.

I looked up to see one of my favorite flight attendants coming toward us with a tray of something. I just thought she was bringing something to the galley behind us. She stopped at our row and offered us four mai tais from First Class in glass glasses. What luxury! The flight attendants came by when they could to chat for a moment, but there is always a lot to do on a Hawaiian flight. They offered beverage services, lunch or dinner service, a halfway to Hawaii quiz type game, and a lot of other things going on. And these were all really good flight attendants that interacted with our customers. I had flown with many of them before. They came by again with some First Class chocolate chip cookies on napkins. We all really felt special and almost like we were in First Class. We were all very appreciative.

When we landed we went shopping for food to bring to the timeshare. Of course we had to get Spam! It's a requirement, right? We stopped by the Macadamia factory and got a bag of crushed macadamia nuts. We rolled chicken in macadamia nuts and barbequed it. It was really good. We also made some rice. The following day we had left over chicken, rice, and spam and threw in some eggs. It was so good. It tasted like Chinese rice. We had fun cooking and then eating outside on the veranda. We took early morning walks in the area and just enjoyed the quiet of that particular area of the island. The flight back was uneventful. I think we got on the first or second flight we tried to stand by for. We may have all sat separately which is common, and I didn't really know the in-flight crew. But that's the way it is. You just never know. But we were sure left with a lovely memorable flight going from San Francisco to Hawaii.

Crew meals are boarded on some long flights for flight attendants. It's in their contract. I used to smile when flight attendants had to bring their crew meals from the First Class cabin all the way back to the Economy section, to be eaten in the galley. The fragrance of their cooked meal (which sometimes was even better than the customer meal that was offered in Economy) would waft through the cabin. They sheepishly took it through the aisles usually covered with a napkin. I mention this because that is what I thought they were doing that day on the Hawaii trip but it turned out to be for the four of us. What a treat.

Then there was the time we went to Europe with another two good friends. Well, they paid for a trip and were full fare "real" passengers. They were going from San Francisco to Houston, Texas, to New York, and then to England, for starters. We decided to go standby (cheaply, well, free) and our plan was to fly from San Francisco to New York and then on to London and meet up with them there. "What do you mean, we haven't booked a hotel room or a rental car, or any excursions?" they asked. They were travelers who liked to have all of their ducks in a row and we flew (as I've mentioned) "seat of the pants." Whatever is going to be is going to be. They were nervous but we convinced them that we'd meet up at some point and then we'd make plans. So we stood by for a flight to New York. We couldn't get on that flight, but we saw a flight that went to Houston, Texas and then on to New York. We landed in Houston, Texas and casually walked over to where they were sitting and surprised them! "What are you doing here?" they asked. "Oh nothing, we were just in the area," we said with straight faces. We visited with them until it was time for them to board their airplane. They got on, of course, and we didn't. "We kept looking for you walking down the aisles. We were so sad when we didn't see you," they later told us. That was okay with us as that is how we roll. Hey, it's free. They got to New York as planned and took the night flight to England. We eventually arrived at the JFK International Airport. We narrowly missed standing by for the last flight of the night out of New York to London. Our inbound trip was slightly delayed. No worries, we'll look for a hotel close by and try again tomorrow. We'll only lose one day we figured. We walked to the baggage claim area where they had (in those days) a lighted board with a bunch of telephones attached to it. You could just pick up one of the phones and talk to the receptionist at the hotel of your choice. Remember those? We started calling hotel after hotel and at some point we realized that there were no rooms to be had. Well, we thought to ourselves, this might be a first for us. Sleeping at the JFK boarding area all night! We had our small bags with us, my handbag and Bill's wallet. Well, it looked safe enough (I guess) but we still decided to take turns sleeping. First, I would sleep and Bill would read or watch those little televisions sets (again in those days) that were attached to the seats. You would put a few coins into the small television sets and you could watch television for a few minutes or a half an hour. Then when I woke up, or when Bill got so tired that he woke me up, it was my turn to read and look out the window while he slept. We felt very protective of one another. It actually went very well. Only once we had to lift our feet off the ground while the janitor vacuumed the rugs under our feet in the wee hours. The next morning at JFK, I saw the sunrise and it was quite beautiful. Believe me I don't see the sunrise very often, especially since I'm now retired. But it was impressive. We were a little rumpled and in need of a shower, but we spruced up in the restroom as best as we could. We stood by for our flight from New York to London. Holy smokes! We got on in First Class! We got to England only eight hours later than our friends. We both got hotel rooms right by Scotland Yard. Once we caught up with them, we rented a car on the spot. No worries, they had cars available. We started driving and stopped along the way whenever we wanted to see a sight or two. Then we thought about getting a room for the next night before getting to our destination. We stopped by maybe one or two hotels before deciding on two hotel rooms for the night. "What if we NEVER find one tonight?" our pals asked. Hey, we had just spent the night in the JFK airport. We are ready for anything. But we easily got our hotel. It was a lovely two-week trip and we traveled all over Europe. When the vacation came to a close, we parted ways to return home. They, with their confirmed seats and itinerary, and us "winging" it with our destinations going towards home -- whatever flight we could get on. I still get a "rush" at not knowing where we'll go and where we will end up. We always eventually get home. We don't know any other way. But if I do buy a real paid for ticket nowadays, I do have a sense of smugness at getting onboard when they say, "now boarding all passengers". That's us!

My sister gave us the remainder of their thirty-year timeshare recently. We had never done a timeshare before because it seemed so restrictive to us. We'd have to be checking in on a specific date in a specific place at a specific time. That's not really us. So when we fly, we might go one day ahead just to be sure we are where we are supposed to be. We have taken only one such trip since we acquired the timeshare and we drove our car! Santa Fe, New Mexico. This was on my bucket list and we went via Sedona, Arizona going (overnight and dinner with friends) and Fountain Hills, Arizona coming back (staying with friends). What a lovely trip it was. We saw some interesting sights along the way. And what a great deal the timeshare destination hotel was. We'll get used to it! We're very thankful for their generosity. Next trip up is a week in Waikiki. Bill will get to surf every day!

We are so grateful that our airline afforded us the time and the opportunity to travel the world. I was looking at a world map the other day and realized just how many places we have been. It would be easier to say where we have not been. We've never been to Russia or Dubai. No reason why not, it just hasn't happened yet. But the sky's the limit. We have our good health to continue traveling to who knows where.

*   *   *   *   *

AFTER THIRTY-THREE YEARS OF ALL OF THIS FUN AND SOME-TIMES VERY HARD WORK, I WAS SITTING IN A MEETING ONE MORN-ING WITH MY BOSS AND MY PEERS. As is sometimes the case with the airline industry, they were looking to lay off some management employees. This time, they said, they would take the most junior management supervisors. I looked around the room at the hopeful up-and- coming supervisors, and their faces had fallen. After the meeting, I spoke to my boss. I said, "Why not let a senior employee take the layoff (like me) and then the youngsters could keep their jobs?" I had worked there all my adult life and was definitely planning to retire at the minimum age of fifty-five anyway. Here was a chance to take "earlier" retirement in the form of a layoff first. I usually discuss this kind of thing with my husband first, but I was in the right place at the right time. I felt so bold asking for this layoff. My boss didn't think the airline would make such an exception. But I asked her if she could please try and just ask her boss. She spoke to her boss that same day and they decided to let me do it. I came home and told my husband what I had done. He was as white as a sheet, but I assured him that we would be all right financially. They were offering me twenty-two months of a leave of absence with zero pay. But they were also offering me medical and dental insurance, pass riding privileges and the right to retire from the leave of absence on October 1, 2004. This would be three days after my fifty-fifth birthday. Bill was working full time at the time, so it worked out very well indeed. Our deal was that I would take a full year off, and on the one-year anniversary of my leave of absence, I would take on a fun, part-time job. "Deal," I said. And I did just that. For that first year not working, I had a ritual that I called working "at the office." I would get my laptop, my purse, and I'd pack a lunch, a sandwich and a soda. I would bring my cellphone with me, and any paperwork I needed to work on. I would drive down to the beach and park the car facing the ocean. There I would make and reschedule appointments, read e-mails, do my banking, pay some bills, or read a book. You get the idea. All the while, I would stop and look out to the ocean and feel very fortunate indeed. Sometimes I would meet friends for lunch or breakfast. Other times I would just putter around the house. I loved being in the routine of working in and on the house, as I had missed it for so many years.

When the year was up, and it went so quickly, I decided to look for a part-time job. I wanted a job that had some sort of art, music, and beautiful colors surrounding me wherever I was going to be. I vowed to do only things that made me happy. I did, and I still do.

I worked for a temporary agency, getting a one-day, two-day, or sometimes a one-week assignment. Then I worked a six-month assignment at City Hall in Half Moon Bay. The art, music, and beautiful colors came along in the form of working at a stunning boutique. The boutique owner came to renew her business license at City Hall. That is how we met. She told me (and I never will forget this), "You look like a flower in a bed of weeds in here." It was almost the end of my six-month assignment and she hired me. Oh my, what a joy to go to work. There was music, art, beautiful items for anyone's home. I loved the job. And it was only a few days a week and for a few hours a day. She was magnificent to work for. She once asked me if I would like to organize the supply and inventory closet. Would I? I was so excited. I get excited over the little things, but I really do love to organize. I started at one end of the closet and organized, labeled, and stacked items beautifully. She also let me take an entire wall of items which were already staged for our customers, and re-do it. "I've had the same display for too long. Surprise me," she said. A couple of years later she saw how much fun I was having being (semi) retired. She decided to close her store and take some much- deserved rest and even move to a new house in a new area. Around that same time, a business owner from across the street, came in to buy candles and she had heard that the boutique was closing. She asked if I would like to come and work for her. Would I! So I started working at a high end Mexican art gallery, with art, sculptures, jewelry, and Latin music. We also hosted an occasional after-hours tequila party in the back room. This owner's ex-husband had a really nice cooking store with cooking classes and high-end cooking items. It was right down the street. So I started helping with that store also. I was "working it" all over Main St., in Half Moon Bay, but never leaning on any lampposts.

Along with some fun part time jobs (yes, there is a life outside of the airline), I started doing local theatre. I was at home one morning with Bill. I was reading the local paper. There were auditions that day in a couple of hours on Main St. at the local theatre. It was after the 9/11 tragedy and I wondered to myself if those people that did not survive the terrorist attack ever got to achieve their hopes and dreams. I decided to go for it. I asked Bill to download a picture for me and I quickly made up a pretty empty resume to take with me. I had been a singer in choirs and had some dance or "moves" that I could claim. I had also performed a few times singing solo. I drove to the theatre, met the director, and got a part. Granted it was a little part, but I got to sing and move with others in the ensemble. I was a maid and I had one line. I said, "Roast Duck?" as I thrust a platter of meat to someone. That became my new "work." I've now been in a dozen or more plays, and recently was in a Lead role. And my ever so sweet first Director said fondly, "I discovered you."

Twenty-two months after I went on my leave of absence, I processed my paperwork to retire officially. Since I had been given a proper send-off at the office (airport) before my leave of absence, I didn't expect anything. I figured my retirement pin would be sent to me in the mail. And of course I would start getting my pension checks!

Then, one night I was doing another play and I heard that seventeen of my former airline co-workers and my former boss were going to be in the audience. How exciting! At the end of the play the audience emptied out, but my co-workers stayed inside the theatre. I ran out to greet them and hug them all. Then we all got onstage (empty now) and they presented me with my retirement pin and paperwork to a round of applause by the seventeen co-workers. How perfect was that! I was beyond thrilled.

I am lucky to still be on stage now and then. I still do a play or two but my real passion is singing. I am a singer in a 60s rock and roll band, The California Cogs. I work with six other talented individuals. Our band-leader, a wonderfully versatile guitarist, is David Davis. In another venue, I also have a duet partner who I call my singing buddy, Donnie. We so enjoy collaborating on different types of music and we both enjoy performing. And we jam with other musicians (my husband included) at least once a week. I'm blessed indeed.

One of our young supervisors was an African-American lady who speaks Dutch and English, if not more languages. She recently told me how when she was a newly hired supervisor, she was seated in the cubicle nearby those of us purser supervisors. I was honored to be a purser super-visor where some (or most) of our flight attendants were the head Purser for a domestic or international flight. She told me how much she learned from all of us. I was so flattered. She's no longer with the airlines, but she has a very wonderful sounding job and does her own share of exciting trav-eling. I was lucky to have breakfast with her several years ago, to catch up with our lives.

When we moved to Oceanside, California after we both retired, we found out that there was a little airport in Carlsbad, California called the Carlsbad Palomar Airport. At the time our airline subsidiary flew out of there, mostly to Los Angeles. They had fifty passenger airplanes and maybe a little larger. But none the size of our big commercial airplanes. What a cute airport to fly into and out of. You basically drove right up to it and parked nearby. You walked into a building with what appeared to be one or two gates. We were planning to stand by for a flight and we had to go through security by walking past one agent and going through the metal detector. He noticed that I had a full sized hairspray container in my purse. He told me he had to confiscate it for security purposes. Of course I gave it to him. He put it on a shelf all by itself. No other items were there. We left the metal detector, took two steps to our gate and another two steps to our seats in the tiny boarding area. It wasn't a particularly full flight so there weren't that many people in the boarding area. The flight was ready for boarding and people walked out a very few feet and walked up a moving staircase to the small aircraft. The boarding agent said, although there were seats available, on this particular day, this flight was weight restricted. This happened often at this airport, we were told. So we could not be boarded. Weight restricted? I had an immediate flashback to TFTF! So we got out of our seats and started to leave once the plane pulled away from the gate. I passed back through security and I motioned to the security agent. I said, "We didn't get on the flight and we're leaving the airport. Can I get my hairspray back?" He grinned and handed it back to me. We got in our car and drove to Los Angeles. We were there in two hours as we had a lot of traffic.

On another trip to Los Angeles from Carlsbad airport, our bags went ahead and we didn't. It was one of those trips that if we made it on that particular flight, we would go to our destination. If we didn't get on, we'd just go home and try again on another day. This was one of those times. We did not get boarded. I called the airport about our two checked bags that went out with the flight and they told me to come by the next day. No problem, we thought, since the airport is only a fifteen minute drive from our home. We drove up the next day and parked almost right in front. We'll only be there for a moment, anyway. We went up to the Baggage Claim area which is again just a few steps from our car. The agent said the bags would be there shortly. We waited for a couple of minutes when a buzzer sounded and a large metal door started to rise up grandly to reveal all of the many bags that were going to be showing up, or so we thought! In the entire baggage claim area, there were only two checked bags coming through – my bag and Bill's bag. Now, that's a small airport!

We had planned to stand by for a flight to Hawaii on another Christmas day. Earlier I mentioned one can more easily get on a flight on the actual holiday because people who are visiting are already there (wherever there is) and they haven't tried to go home yet. For some odd reason, we knew the flight was from Los Angeles to Hawaii, but we decided to drive down to San Diego airport. We had planned to take the morning flight from San Diego to Los Angeles and be in place for the Los Angeles to Honolulu flight. By this time our airline subsidiary was no longer flying out of Palomar airport. We were on the airplane so early that it was too early to take off. We had to sit there until the curfew was up. So we sat and sat. When we finally got to Los Angeles we did not go to a gate but instead sat on the tarmac. The skeleton crew of customer service agents on that holiday was such that we couldn't get to our gates. No one was available to pull up the jetway. We looked at our watches. We had missed the Los Angeles to Honolulu flight that we had planned to stand by for, and still we sat on the tarmac. Then we watched the second Los Angeles to Honolulu flight leave for its destination. Nothing we could do but sit there. People were yelling (what good will that do?), a few were crying because they were missing their Christmas day. When we could we just texted our hosts and told them we'd let them know when we were on the plane. Then the agent arrived, opened the door, and let us out. We went to stand by for our third attempt at the flight and we got on. We had planned to be at the Honolulu airport around 11:00 a.m. but instead we arrived around 5:00 p.m. No worries. Our host picked us up, took us to their home, and his thoughtful wife had

Christmas dinner ready and waiting for us – Christmas in Waikiki. We had a wonderful stay with them.

In retirement, when we are not traveling, we can still be found around airports. We now occasionally go to Sunday brunch at The Landings, a wonderful restaurant that is located right in the Palomar Carlsbad Airport. This restaurant is owned by a retired airline employee -- a former flight attendant. We met recently, and we know some of the same people. This is amazing, because she worked out of Los Angeles and I worked out of San Francisco. There are thousands and thousands of airline employees. It's a small world indeed.

We have brunch there when our new friends perform. They are the Chris Fast Band, with our dear friend on upright bass. We so enjoy listening to them. They are all such very good musicians. We can usually be found sitting outside on a beautiful southern California day with friends and acquaintances, listening to them. We'll watch the occasional (very occasional) airplane or corporate jet come in, land, deplane passengers, get serviced, and go back out again, all the while listening to some great blues music.

With all that is going on in this crazy world today, I still always look on the bright side of almost everything. I admit that I am an optimist. I can't help it, I'm just a glass half-full kind of gal. But we are still having an amazing life, and we have been able to do so much traveling and fun shenanigans. We're now 68 and 69 years young respectively and we have our good health. What more could you ask for in life? We are truly blessed.

Of course, it was not all fun and games. Yes, there was the rare (but horrific) events that occurred over the years. There was the unbelievable 9/11 terrorist attack which left employees, customers, and loved ones devastated. We had the rare airplane incident (we have, however, an excellent maintenance record), the power outages, trip cancellations, bad weather, and delays. But the best times stand out the most. I am so grateful for the airline who hired me as a child of nineteen, and enabled me to help pay for a few homes, cars, and racing hobbies, and to have wonderful memories of flying to many places in the world. I still think of my workplace (and I say a grateful thank you) when I get my precious pensions each month. I am grateful that I'm able to keep paying for my medical insurance from them. And for thirty-three of those working years, I had full company paid medical insurance – I didn't pay a dime.

Oh, and did I mention that Bill and I still get unlimited free space available privileges for the rest of our lives? We do.

I retired at age fifty-five. It was (and is) a great ride!

THE END